Quick and Easy Ways With RIBBON
Ceci Johnson

TECHNIQUES FOR WOVEN-EDGE RIBBON —
IDEAS AND PROJECTS FOR CLOTHING, CRAFTS,
HOME DECORATION, AND GIFTS

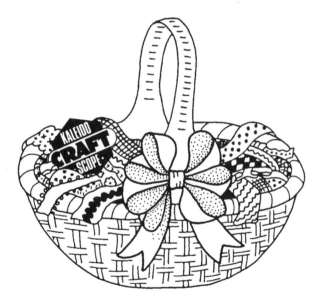

CHILTON BOOK COMPANY
RADNOR, PENNSYLVANIA

D1122219

Acknowledgments

I am grateful to the following people and companies who provided information and samples for use in preparing this book:

Dale Nicholson of Lion Ribbon Company for wire-edge, novelties, and tulles;

Joellen Reinhardt of William E. Wright Company, for satin and grosgrain;

Scott Blackham of Y.L.I. Corporation, for Japanese silk ribbon;

Liz Dircksen of Angelsea, for samples of vintage ribbons;

Sue Hausmann of Viking Sewing Machines for permission to use Erica's Bow.

Thank you to American Crafters Outlet, Bedford Bendable, Elsie's Exquisiques, Falk Industries, Grayblock Ribbon Mills, Karen's Kreations, C.M. Offray & Son, Viv's Ribbons & Laces, and Sopp America for sending catalogs and other information.

Thank you to Yvonne Perez-Collins for ideas and encouragement, as well as the ribbon samples she painted.

I also appreciate my local fabric stores—House of Fabrics, Fabricland, and Hancock Fabrics—for always having a sale right when I needed one.

Thank you to Rosalie Cooke, Martha Vercoutere, and the folks at Chilton for your expertise and assistance to bring this book to its final form.

I am grateful to Robbie Fanning, for the inspiration her books and other writings have given me over the years—also for her creativity, encouragement, expertise, and the seed of an idea for this book. It is a joy to work with her.

I am grateful to my mother, Alberta Humphreys, for encouragement and the gift of loving a needle and thread.

I am especially grateful to my husband and best friend, Bill, for his confidence in everything I do—also for his patience with upheaval in the household while I'm busy pursuing projects like this book.

Thank you to you, fellow creative person, for taking on the challenge of learning new ideas and expanding your universe.

Copyright © 1993 by Ceci Johnson

All Rights Reserved

Published in Radnor, Pennsylvania 19089, by Chilton Book Company

No part of this book may be reproduced, transmitted or stored in any form or by any means, electronic or mechanical, without prior written permission from the publisher.

Designed by Martha Vercoutere

Drawings by Ceci Johnson

Color photographs by Lee Lindeman and Mark Jenkins

Design of color pages by Anthony Jacobson

Edited by Robbie Fanning and Rosalie Cooke

Production by Rosalie Cooke and Gil Bowers

Library of Congress Cataloging-in-Publication Data

Johnson, Ceci.
    Quick and easy ways with ribbon / Ceci Johnson.

    p. cm. — (Craft kaleidoscope)
    Includes bibliographical references and index.
    ISBN 0-8019-8498-X
    1. Ribbon work. I. Title. II. Series.
TT850.5.J64 1993
746'.0476—dc20   93-8198
                                        CIP

1 2 3 4 5 6 7 8 9 0   2 1 0 9 8 7 6 5 4 3

Table of Contents

Foreword

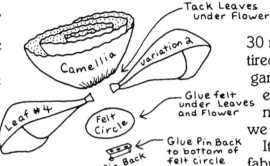

Tack Leaves Under Flower

Camellia

Variation 2

Leaf #4

Glue felt under Leaves and Flower

Felt Circle

Glue Pin Back to bottom of felt circle

Pin Back

As a confirmed fabric fancier, I have a new love: wire-edge ribbon. One of the woven-edge ribbons Ceci Johnson covers in this wonderful book, wire-edge ribbon has a thin copper wire woven into each side. That means you can bend it, pleat it, roll it, even gather it along the wire—and it maintains its shape.

For a working person like me, it's a blessing. Last night during the commercials of my favorite half-hour TV show, I made my mother a wire-edge camellia. This morning before work, I made two velvet wire-edge leaves—in 10 minutes! Tonight I'll sew a pinback to a small circle of felt, attach the two leaves, and tack the camellia over them. In less than an hour's work, I'll have a special corsage for her birthday.

Wire-edge are not the only ribbons I'm playing with. I have a basket of silk, satin, taffeta, grosgrain, velvet, and others in the living room, along with basic sewing supplies. They have revitalized my evenings.

For some time, I've wanted to do some handwork at night while I watch TV, so I don't feel like a total couch potato. But I'm usually too pooped to start anything. Ribbons, however, are perfect. I've covered a small cardboard bolt from the fabric store with batting and cotton ribbing. I'm working my way through Chapter 6, Ribbon Flowers, and as I finish each one, I pin it to the bolt.

Because I see results so quickly, especially working with wire-edge ribbon— 5 minutes, 10 minutes, 30 minutes—I forget that I'm tired. When I look at my garden of ribbons, I experience one of those quiet moments of satisfaction that we all cherish.

It's given my jaunts to the fabric store a new focus, too. For $3 - $10, I can buy yards and evenings of pleasure. This raises an interesting question, though. If a ribbon is a length of woven material finished on both sides, at what width does a ribbon cease to be a ribbon and become yardage?

Now that my attention has been narrowed to ribbon width, I'm calling my entire fabric stash The Ribbon Collection. Some ribbons are 1/4" wide; some are 45".

I hope you'll revitalize your days and evenings, too, with the help of this charming book.

Robbie Fanning
Series Editor

Are you interested in a quarterly newsletter about creative uses of the sewing machine and serger, edited by Robbie Fanning? Write to The Creative Machine, PO Box 2634-B, Menlo Park, CA 94026.

Preface

Until the summer of 1991, my trips to the fabric store usually included a stop at the ribbon counter to admire the shine of the satins, the intensity of the grosgrains, and the bits of gold and silver in the brocades. I loved to turn tapestry ribbons over and marvel at all those tiny threads it took to put a pretty little rose or other motif on the front of the ribbon. I would pull a spool off the display, unroll a length of ribbon over my hand, and think how I would take home yards and yards and "do something" with them. I would then carefully rewind the ribbon and put it back in the display because, in reality, I had not a clue what I would do with the ribbon once I got it home.

Things changed in the summer of 1991. Robbie Fanning introduced me to an old ribbon text. In the pages of the old book, I found techniques that made all those spools of ribbon come alive. I hurried to the fabric store and bought a few yards of red grosgrain and pink satin ribbon. I came home and dug in. Although the text's instructions and pictures were cryptic and some of the recommended uses for ribbon were dated,

the techniques made my yards of ribbon come alive with dimension and texture. I was hooked. I have not been able to pass a ribbon counter since without taking several ribbons home with me.

I spent the summer playing with the techniques in the old book and playing the game of "what if?" with ribbon—what if I folded it this way or tacked it that way? What if I combined this and that? And so, this book was born. It presents many old techniques and some new twists as well. Its purpose is to thrill you, excite you, and stir your imagination—through satin and taffeta, grosgrain, silk, and brocade.

On a more "tangible" level, the book has these objectives:

1. *To present timeless ribbon techniques in a way that is understandable to today's needleworker/crafter.* I have tried to present each technique with sufficient diagrams and instructions to let you easily learn it, no matter what your skill level.

2. *To adapt old techniques to the beautiful ribbons readily available today.* All projects and techniques call for ribbons readily available in

my local fabric stores, so they should be available in most places. Choose the readily available ribbons or order imported and vintage ribbons from the companies listed in the Sources of Supply on page 87.

3. *To present creative ways to use ribbon on items we enjoy today.* Suggested uses are based on items currently available and in use, including both hand- and ready-made items.

4. *To make ribbon work fast and fun, without sacrificing any of its beauty.* Our busy lives often leave limited time for sewing and crafts. Most projects are designed to be completed in an evening or two.

5. *To give us all a reason to bring home those gorgeous ribbons.* Yardages are suggested for techniques and projects so you will quickly get started in ribbon work.

Approach this book with a playful spirit and let your imagination soar.

I'll be looking for you at the ribbon counter.

Ceci Johnson
Clovis, California

Decorating With Ribbon

Clothing

Skirts
Blouses
Aprons
Lingerie
Nighties & Robes
Dresses
Vests
Sweaters
Jackets
T-Shirts
Sweatshirts
Jeans & Slacks
Jumpsuits
Children's Clothes

Parts of Clothing to Decorate

Collars
Cuffs
Plackets
Pockets
Hems
Bodices
Yokes
Necklines
Front openings
Back openings
Waistlines
Shoulders
Sleeves

Home Accessories

Placemats & Napkins
Napkin Rings
Table Cloths & Runners
Coasters
Quilts & Comforters
Sheets and Pillow Cases
Throw Pillows
Lampshades
Curtains
Guest, Tea & Bath Towels
Picture Frames & Mirrors
Photo Albums
Jewelry Boxes
Baskets
Hangers
Sachets
Flower Pots
Containers & Holders
Chatelaines
Pin Cushions
Sewing Baskets
Book Covers & Bookmarks
Doll Clothes

Personal Accessories

Totes
Evening Bags
Purses
Barrettes
Hair Bows
Hats
Headbands
Bracelets
Necklaces
Pins
Earrings
Sandals
Shoes
Slippers
Belts & Sashes
Garters

Decorating for Special Occasions

Holidays & Special Occasions

Christmas
New Year's
Valentine's Day
St. Patrick's Day
Mother's Day
Easter
Fourth of July
Halloween
Thanksgiving
Weddings
Anniversaries
Birthdays
Bridal/Baby Showers
Baptisms & Christenings
Family Reunions
House Warmings
Open Houses

What to Decorate

Party Clothes
Gift Packaging
Invitations
Party Favors
Table Accessories
Centerpieces
Nametags & Placecards
Door & Window Decoration
Baskets
Bouquets
Ornaments

1. Introducing Ribbon

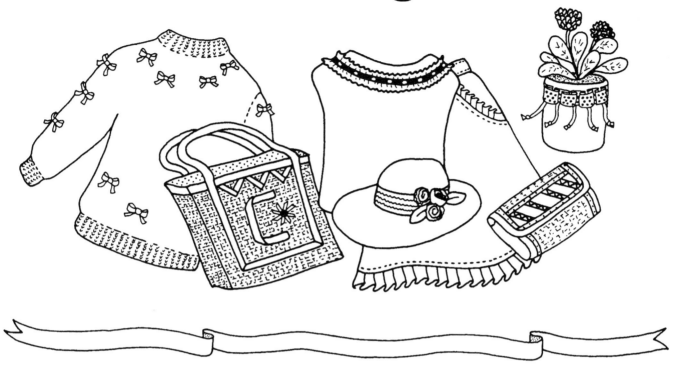

Decorate, embellish, and adorn anything and everything with ribbon. It's versatile and fun to work with. It adds a beautiful finish to home-crafted projects and spices up ready-made items with a personalized touch. The charts on the opposite page provide a taste of what ribbon can embellish.

Ribbon can be pleated, gathered, applied in bands, folded, woven, rolled, and more. Other embellishments such as laces, eyelet ruffles, buttons, beads, braids, rick rack, tiny bows and flowers, fabric paints, and machine and hand embroidery can be added.

This book will introduce you to the basic techniques for woven-edge ribbon. After learning these techniques, endless possibilities for ex-panding and combining them will be yours. I warn you—ribbon manipulation can be habit-forming.

For those anxious to get started: If you're familiar with ribbon, have some at home, and want to get started right now, several charts will help you choose a starting point. Turn to "Choosing Ribbons for Each Technique" (see pages 4 and 5) to help you match your ribbons to appropriate tech-niques. If you seek projects, refer to the "Time Estimates" chart (see page 11) to find ones that fit your time con-straints.

Ribbon Terms and Details

Figure 1.1 shows the various parts of a length of ribbon and the illustration details that will be used throughout the book. It also demonstrates three folds which are commonly used in manipulating ribbon.

A term that deserves special mention is **face**. Ribbon, like any fabric, has two sides. The right, or usable, side of a length of ribbon is called the **face**. A ribbon with one usable side is called **single-face** ribbon, and one with both sides usable is called **double-face**. The term is most commonly associated with satin ribbon, since it is available in single- and double-face varieties.

Types of Ribbon

Ribbon comes in several types for different purposes.

Woven-Edge Ribbon is woven and has woven edges. It is supple and drapeable, like sewing fabrics. It is suitable for clothing, as well as for accessories, home decoration, and crafts. It is most often washable, although sometimes may require dry-cleaning. It is sometimes called Apparel Ribbon.

Craft Ribbon can be woven or non-woven. If woven, it usually has a cut, rather than woven, edge and is stiffer because it is treated to retard ravelling. Craft ribbon is not suitable for clothing and other washables, but makes wonderfully loopy bows and other adornments for baskets, floral arrangements, and other

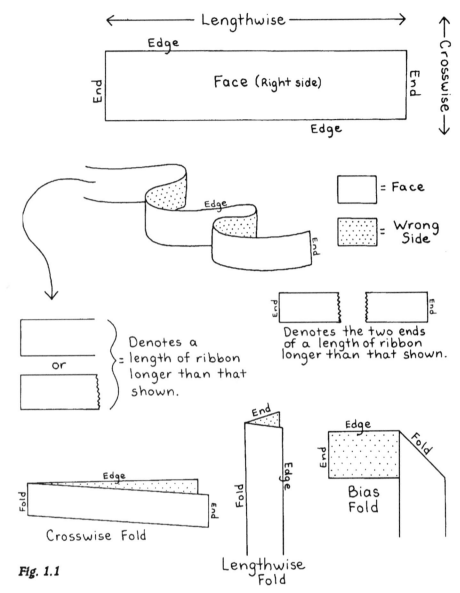

Fig. 1.1

crafts. *This book will concentrate on woven-edge ribbon* and its many uses for clothing, accessories, home decoration, and craft projects. This does not mean craft ribbons are off-limits, but just that most craft ribbons will not have the suppleness needed for the techniques shown. If you find one that works for a particular technique, use it. The main thing is to know what kind of ribbon you are getting and that it will be suitable, in terms

of washability and wear, for the project at hand.

Is It Woven-Edge or Craft Ribbon?

From a distance, and sometimes even up close, woven-edge and craft ribbon look similar. Check the feel of the ribbon and read labels. If the label doesn't specify which kind of ribbon it is, look for care instructions. If instructions on how to wash or dry-

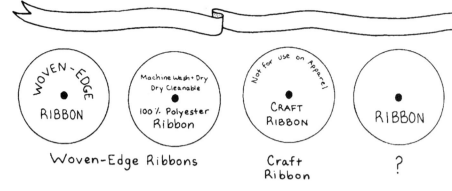

Fig. 1.2 Reading labels is the first step in determining if a ribbon is suitable for a project.

clean the ribbon are given, the ribbon is woven-edge. (Figure 1.2.)

If the label does not provide the answer, check the edges to see how they are finished.

The woven edge is usually fairly distinctive. Check, too, the suppleness of the ribbon. If it has a drapeability similar to sewing fabric, it is probably woven-edge, or at least usable for the techniques in this book as if it were woven-edge. Without care instructions, however, I would not permanently attach it to anything that will require washing or dry cleaning.

Woven-Edge Ribbon

Most woven-edge ribbons available today are 100% polyester. Some use nylon or other synthetics. The easy-care washability and suppleness of these ribbons makes them suitable for a wide range of uses. Always check for care instructions on the spool when purchasing ribbon.

Ribbons like those available earlier in the 20th century are becoming more readily available again today. Most are imported from France or Japan. Specialty Retailers (see Sources of Supply) carry a variety of vintage ribbons in silk and synthetics.

Varieties of Woven-Edge Ribbon

Woven-edge ribbons are classified by fabric type. Study the samplers shown in the color photographs of the basic varieties and the novelty ribbons available. Learn about each variety from the descriptions that follow. Then take a trip to the fabric store to read labels and identify each. I defy you to get out of the store without purchasing ribbon.

A. Grosgrain Ribbon has a distinct ribbed texture running from edge to edge. It has body, or substance, and usually both faces are usable. This is often true even if one face has a printed pattern. Interesting effects result from using the differences in the faces. (See Figure 2.18 on page 19.) Grosgrain ribbon is commonly available in widths from 3/8" to 2-1/4". See its use on the Christmas Bell Pull on page 45 and the primrose on page 67.

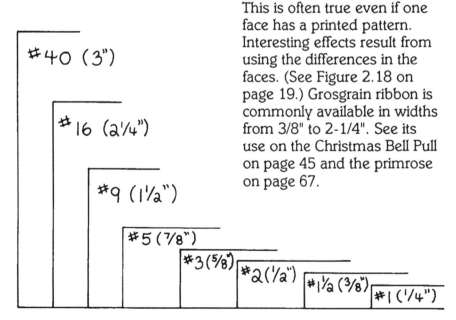

Fig. 1.3 Ribbon manufacturers use a numbering system to designate ribbon widths. The corresponding width in inches is given.

B. Satin Ribbon has a smooth surface and lustrous shine. Satin can be single-face, with only one side shiny, or double-face, with both sides shiny. Double-face satin has more body than single-face. Satin ribbon is commonly available in widths from 1/16" to 3". Make beautiful satin bows like the Rose Bow on page 53.

C. Taffeta Ribbon has a plain weave with a smooth surface and characteristic sheen. It can have body or be delicate in weight. Some are best described as having a crisp feel, and others a soft feel. Look for **Moiré** taffeta, shown on the sampler, with its elegant, "watermarked" pattern. Taffeta widths range from 1/16" for the tiniest silk, to 2" wide for synthetics. Taffeta trims the Good Morning Placemats and Napkin Rings on page 23, and the Heart Sachet on page 34.

D. Jacquard-Loomed Ribbons include three kinds so named for the type of loom used to make them. They have patterns and motifs woven into the face and come in many widths. Since they often contain a variety of fibers, check care instructions carefully. All kinds of jacquard-loomed ribbons make elegant Pump Bows (page 51). Brocade is used for the "I Love a Brocade" ornament on page 12.

1. Tapestry Ribbon is single-face because the threads that decorate the face are carried along the back between motifs.

Choosing Ribbons for Each Technique

Ribbon Variety	Straight Borders	Mitered Borders	Folded Borders
Grosgrain	Excellent	Excellent	Excellent
Satin	Excellent	Excellent	Double-face: Excellent Single-face: No
Taffeta	Excellent	Excellent	Excellent
Sheers	No	No	No
Jacquards	Excellent	Excellent	Double-face: Excellent Single-face: No
Velvet	Excellent	No	Double-face: Suitable
Metallic Novelties	Excellent	Suitable	Double-face: Suitable

Ribbon Variety	Gathers	Pleats	Best Bows
Grosgrain	Suitable	Excellent	Traditional, Tied, Pump, Gathered Bows
Satin	Excellent	Excellent	All bows
Taffeta	Excellent	Excellent	Traditional, Tied, Rose Bows
Sheers	Excellent	No	Tied, Rose Bows
Jacquards	No	Double Face: Suitable	Pump Bows
Velvet	No	No	Pump Bows
Metallic Novelties	No	Excellent	Sheer ones: Rose, Tied Bow. Heavier ones: Pump Bows

Unless these contain a lot of metallic fibers, they are often more supple than the other two varieties.

2. Jacquard Ribbon is double-face, with the pattern on each face reversed.

The Jacquard on the sampler shows both sides of the ribbon so the pattern reversal is evident.

3. Brocade Ribbon has a raised textural effect. It is also single-face. Metallic threads and floral and scroll motifs abound on brocades. They tend to be stiffer than either of the other Jacquards.

Choosing Ribbons for Each Technique (Con't.)

Ribbon Variety	Best Flowers	Other Techniques
Grosgrain	Poppy, Primrose, Sunflower, Rolled Loop Daisy	Ribbon Drawing Weaving Knotted Ribbon Ribbon Button
Satin	Roses, Sweet Pea, Spring Blossom, Knotted Daisy, Dahlia	Double-Face: Excellent Ribbon Drawing Ribbon Button Single-Face: Suitable Weaving Knotted Ribbon
Taffeta	Spring Blossom, Sweet Pea, Poppy, Wire-Edge Camellia	Ribbon Drawing Weaving Ribbon Button
Sheers	Camellia	
Jacquards	None	Use narrow ones as accents in weaving
Velvet	Rolled Loop Daisy	
Metallic Novelties	Varies depending on the ribbon's weight and suppleness	

Key:
　　Excellent: Good choice, most ribbons in the variety work well with the technique.
　　Suitable: Many ribbons in the variety can be used but results will vary.
　　No: Most ribbons of the variety will not give satisfactory results.

E. Sheer Ribbons are made of thin, almost transparent nylon, polyester, or other synthetics. They are usually very soft and drapeable. Some have monofilament woven into the edges, which helps them keep a shape such as loops for bows. Sheers tend to be wider ribbons, often 1-1/2" and up. Make exuberant Rose Bows (see page 53) with sheers.

F. Velvet Ribbon has soft nap on its face. It has considerable substance due to the nap. It is commonly found, single-face, in widths from 3/8" to 7/8". Specialty sources can provide wider velvets, as well as double-face ones. Velvet ribbon trims the Bow Angel's dress on page 59 and makes the petals of the Rolled Loop Daisy on page 71.

G. Novelty Ribbons are represented in the color photographs with their own sampler. Shown are but a few of the many available. Novelties include ribbons that don't fit neatly in one of the other categories because they combine several varieties in one ribbon. They also include those that combine unusual materials and surface effects, ribbons in which metallic or iridescent threads predominate, and ready-made pleated, gathered, wrinkled, or curled ribbons. Try a Camellia on page 65, using ready-made pleated ribbon. Adorn the Bow Angel on page 59 with metallic wings.

Edge Treatments on Woven-Edge Ribbon

The edges of ribbon often receive special treatment. Two special edge treatments are most commonly available.

Picot-Edge features a prominent, decorative looped edge. It is found most often on taffeta ribbon, but can sometimes also be found on satin, velvet, and even Jacquards.

Feather-Edge features a delicate looped edge of finer threads than picot. It is most often found on narrow (3/16" to 5/8") double-face satin ribbons.

Other edge treatments include lace, scallops, and crochet. Samples of feather, picot, and crochet edges are shown in the color photographs.

Another popular edge treatment is **Wire-Edge** ribbon. This ribbon has a thin wire, usually copper, woven into each edge, which allows the ribbon to be easily bent into a loop or other shape and stay that way. It is wonderful for bows, flowers, and novelty pleats. When cutting wire-edge ribbons, use all-purpose scissors, not your best pair, as the wire can dull or pit scissor blades.

A green **ombré** wire-edge bow is shown in the color photographs with the other edge treatments. Ombré refers to ribbons variegated from light to dark or from one color to another.

Designing Unique Ribbons

Sometimes it is fun to create an entirely unique ribbon. A sampler of some one-of-a-kind ribbons is shown in the color photographs. Here are some ideas for creating your own ribbons:

1. Combine two ribbons, ribbon and lace, or ribbon and other trims.

2. Add decorative machine- or hand-stitches to the face.

3. Embellish the edges with lace, trims, needlelace, crochet, or decorative machine stitches.

4. Paint the face of the ribbon with fabric paints or pens.

Yvonne Perez-Collins painted white grosgrain ribbon with fabric pens for the sample in the color photograph.

Selecting Ribbon

When planning a project and shopping for its ribbon, ask yourself these questions to help choose from the many selections available.

1. Is the ribbon suitable for the project?
a. What care will the finished project or garment require?
Sewing a dry-clean-only brocade on a bath towel may not be the best choice.

b. What kind of use will the finished project get?
A delicate satin will quickly lose its luster on children's play clothes. It is, however, an appropriate choice for a party dress.

2. Is the ribbon suitable for the technique?
a. Does the ribbon have the characteristics I need for the techniques I will use?
Refer to the chart called "Choosing Ribbons for Each Technique" on pages 4 and 5 for some general guidelines on which ribbons work best for each technique. For example, jacquards usually do not gather well. A single-face satin, however, gathers beautifully.

b. Do I need single- or double-face ribbon?
As a general rule, where only one side of the ribbon will be prominently displayed on the end product, single-face ribbon is adequate.

3. Am I buying enough ribbon for the technique and size of the project?
Be generous. Always add extra—for ease, for miscalculations, and for making samples. There is nothing worse than running 2" short on a beautiful embellishment.

Caring for Woven-Edge Ribbon

Storage
Coiled ribbon will store better than folded ribbon. (Figure 1.4.) Over time, folded ribbon develops creases that may never fully come out. Store ribbon on the cardboard spool from the store, or make your own spools. To make

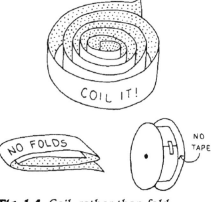

Fig. 1.4 Coil, rather than fold, ribbon. Folding often results in hard to remove creases. Avoid using tape on spools.

spools, cut cardboard rolls, such as those from paper towels, to the width of the ribbon it is to hold. Glue a circle of thin cardboard on each end with white glue or hot-melt glue. (Figure 1.5.)

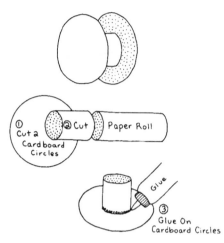

Fig. 1.5 *Homemade spools protect ribbon for storage.*

Tape is often used on spools to keep ribbon from uncoiling. With time, the adhesive on the tape can leave a mark not only on the end, but on several layers of ribbon under it. To keep a spool from uncoiling, cut a strip of clingy plastic wrap the width of the ribbon and wrap it around the outside of the ribbon on the spool, overlapping its ends so they cling together.

Preshrinking
Any washable ribbon or trim for use on a washable item should be preshrunk. Do this even if the care instructions say it does not need preshrinking.

To prevent a long length of ribbon from becoming tangled in the washer and dryer, coil it, place it in a knee-high stocking and loosely knot the top of the stocking.

Pressing
Ribbons have delicate faces easily marred by hot irons and heavy pressure. Press only if there is a reason to, use the lowest setting that will work, and be quick and gentle.

Susan Sirkis, in her video *The Art of Ribbon Craft,* (See Bibliography) suggests a great way to remove creases from ribbon. Stand the iron on its heel and pass the ribbon length quickly across the soleplate of the iron several times. If more pressure is needed, place the iron with the soleplate down on the ironing board and quickly pull the ribbon length through between the iron and board. (Figure 1.6.)

Where a hotter iron is needed to bond fusibles, press out stubborn wrinkles, or remove distortion caused by embroidering on ribbon, cover the face of the ribbon with a press cloth.

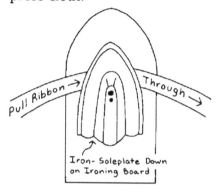

Fig. 1.6 *To press ribbon, set the iron soleplate down on an ironing board. Pull ribbon through quickly between the soleplate and ironing board.*

Working With Woven-Edge Ribbon

Making Samples
There are five times to make samples:

1. To learn a new technique.

2. To try a technique you already know on a different ribbon.

3. To test a new way of attaching a particular ribbon.

4. Before making a project. Use all of the materials to be used on the final project, in the same way they will be used.

5. Anytime you are unsure of the results.

It is always better to work the bugs out on a sample than to ruin a project.

Dealing With Raw Ends
Every length of ribbon has two raw ends. To prevent them from raveling, there are several alternatives depending on the end use of the ribbon.

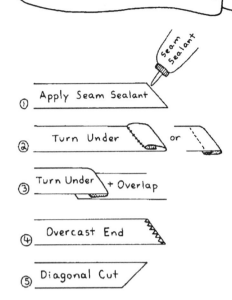

①	Apply Seam Sealant
②	Turn Under or
③	Turn Under + Overlap
④	Overcast End
⑤	Diagonal Cut

Fig. 1.7 Finishing raw ends.

Some alternatives, shown in Figure 1.7, above.

1. Treat the ends with a seam sealant, such as Fray Check, or rub white glue (washable glue if needed) into the thread ends.

2. Turn ends under once or twice and machine or hand stitch.

3. Turn one end under and overlap it on top of the other end.

4. Overcast the raw ends by hand or with a machine zigzag stitch.

5. Cut the ends on the diagonal.

Pinning and Basting

Test pin and baste a sample to see if permanent marks will remain. Try not to pin or baste far in advance of final application. The longer pins and basting remain in ribbon, the more chance for damage.

Fig. 1.8 Cut ribbon on glass with a low-watt soldering iron to simultaneously cut and seal raw ends.

To pin, use 1" long size 16 pleat pins or 1-1/16" long size 17 silk pins, available in fabric stores. These are finer than other pins. Use as few pins as possible without sacrificing accuracy of placement.

To baste, use sewing thread and needles with small eyes, such as quilting or between needles.

Adhesive basting products are available to help hold ribbon in place for sewing. I like Therm O Web's HeatnBond Lite, a sewable iron-on adhesive, to hold straight band borders. There are other brands, too. Be sure to test any brand on a sample first to see that it gives the desired results.

Adhesive basting tapes, such as Collins' Quilter's 1/4" Tape are sometimes helpful. Because ribbons are delicate, I use these tapes only on the back or ends of ribbon. These tapes are not usually intended to be ironed or sewn through. Collins' Wash-A-Way Wonder Tape is one exception. It is a double-sided adhesive tape that can be sewn. After stitching, wash the tape away with water.

Other alternatives for quick holding are glue sticks or spray and liquid light-adhesive products.

Application Methods

Sewn Applications

Machine stitching: Unless the ribbon or foundation fabric is heavy, use size 60, 65, or 70 (American Size 8, 9, 10) needles for machine stitching ribbon. These are made for sewing lightweight fabrics. Except for gathering, use a short to medium stitch length.

Hand stitching: Use a needle with a small eye, such as a quilting needle or between. Stitch with blind stitches (see Figure 2.5 on page 14), watching the stitch tension to ensure the ribbon does not become warped.

No-Sew Applications

The variety of glues, fusibles, and other adhesives currently on the market is mind-boggling. Each has its advantages and drawbacks. Some can change the character of the ribbon and stiffen it. Read labels and test, test, test.

Glues: White craft glue, such as Aleene's Tacky, is my favorite for applying flat bands of ribbon to baskets and other craft projects. When ribbon is attached to washable items, be sure to use a washable glue, such as Aleene's Ok to Wash It.

Hot-melt glues, especially the low-temperature ones, are handy for attaching bows and flowers to baskets, hatbands, and such. They can be a little too thick and quick drying for applying flat bands.

Iron-on adhesives: These products are helpful for attaching flat bands of ribbon. Look for ones such as HeatnBond Ultra Hold, Pellon's Wonder-Under, and Beacon's Liqui-Fuse (a liquid iron-on adhesive) that are permanent and washable without machine stitching.

Making Items Detachable

For items such as a bow or flower that are best detached from a garment before washing, use rustproof safety pins or easily removed hand stitching. Use 26- or 28-gauge floral or brass wire to tie bows and flowers to baskets. Don't overlook hook-and-loop tapes, such as Velcro, too.

Handy Equipment for Working With Ribbon

In addition to items already mentioned, here are a few more that make ribbon work fast and easy. Check your local fabric and craft stores for the suggested supplies. Most are also available from the mail-order companies listed in the Sources of Supply on page 87.

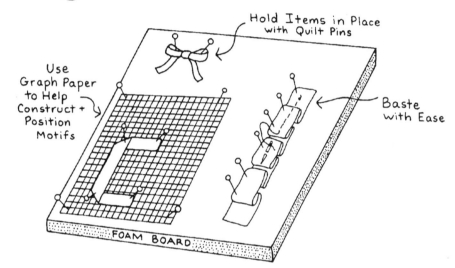

Fig. 1.9 A foam-board pin board is a versatile tool.

Foam-Board Pin Board

Pin ribbon to a board as you work for greater freedom when manipulating considerable lengths or working something complex. My most used tool for working with ribbon is, quite simply, a piece of foam board, such as Monsanto's Fome Cor. It consists of 3/16"-thick foam sandwiched between two paper surfaces. It is inexpensive and available in various sizes from art, office, and craft stores. The sizes it comes in are often bigger than desired for a pin board, but it is easily cut with a straight edge and mat knife. My favorite pin boards are 6" x 8" and a 12" square.

Pin a piece of graph paper to the board and it becomes an indispensable tool for planning motifs and intricate ribbon designs. (Figure 1.9.) Tack layers of ribbon together for basting, then easily scoop your basting needle through all layers without problem. On cloth boards it is easy to catch the cloth in the basting.

Press Board

A cloth-covered press board is handy for pressing without putting up the ironing board. Several commercial boards have printed grids. Look for various models of table-top ironing boards as well.

Clear Plastic Ruler

A clear plastic ruler with 1/8" grid markings is essential for measuring in all sewing and craft work. These are available at office, art, craft, and fabric stores. Choose one at least 12" long and 2" wide.

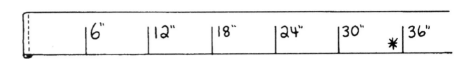

Ribbon Estimating Tape

Make a 3-1/2 yard long "Ribbon Estimating Tape," marked off in 6" increments, to help determine how much ribbon is needed for a project. (Figure 1.10.) In chapter 5, we

Markings: 6, 12, 18, 24, 30, 36*, 42, 48, 54, 60, 66, 72**,

78, 84, 90, 96, 102, 108***, 114, 120, 126.

Fig. 1.11 Use a fine line fabric paint bottle to mark the Ribbon Estimating Tape at 6" intervals. Mark each yard with asterisks.

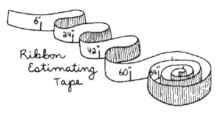

Fig. 1.10 A homemade Ribbon Estimating Tape is handy to estimate the amount of ribbon needed for bows, pleats and folded borders.

will see its use to estimate ribbon for a bow by actually making a quick prototype of the bow, in hand, with the tape. (See Figure 5.2 on page 47.)

Supplies:
3-1/2 yards of 7/8"-wide grosgrain
Fabric paint in a bottle with a fine line tip, dark color
Tape measure or ruler

1. Finish the ribbon ends by turning them under and stitching across the ribbon.

2. Using a tape measure or ruler and a pencil, mark the entire length of the ribbon in 6" increments.

3. Using the fabric paint, make a line at each 6" mark and write the measurement, as shown in Figure 1.11. Use asterisks to designate each yard marking as well.

Measuring Tape

This sewing staple is handy for accurately measuring around an item to determine how much ribbon to use and for measuring long lengths of ribbon. Choose the longest one you can find—mine is 120" long.

Quilt Pins

These pins are 1-1/2" long with a bead at the top. While pleat or silk pins are used to pin ribbon layers together, quilt pins are great for tacking things to the foam-board pin board. They are also useful for coaxing ribbon into place. (See Figure 3.21 on page 32.)

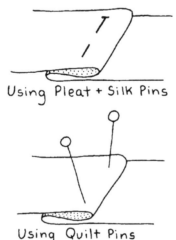

Fig. 1.12 Pleat and silk pins pin layers of ribbon together. Quilt pins are the best choice to tack ribbon to a pin board.

Clips

To lend an extra hand when working with ribbon, California ribbon artist Candace Kling suggests using long bobby pins or hair curl clips to hold ribbon. My favorite are the curl clips.

Using Curl Clips

Fig. 1.13 Hair curl clips hold layers of ribbon together.

Stabilizers

Stabilizers retard distortion of ribbon when embroidering on its face. My favorite stabilizers for ribbon are liquid ones, such as Palmer/Pletsch Perfect Sew. Spray starch can also be used. Saturate the ribbon with stabilizer or starch and let it dry. Wash it out after the embroidery is completed.

The Scrap Basket

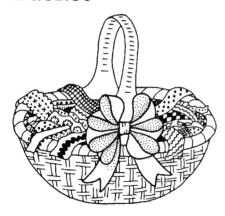

Fig. 1.14 *Store bits of leftover ribbon in a scrap basket decorated with ribbon.*

This is an essential. Keep a basket or box filled with bits of left-over ribbon. I keep any length 2" or longer, plus any projects or samples that just didn't turn out right. These make good test ribbons and also come in handy when a bit of ribbon is needed to make such things as a tiny bow, flower, or center wrap for a bow. It is amazing how many times I dig into my scraps and find just the right piece. See my ribbon-decorated scrap basket in the color photographs.

Let's Get Started...

It's time to get busy and play with some ribbon. The next six chapters cover a variety of ribbon techniques. Basic techniques are shown, along with variations and ideas for using what you have learned. Each chapter, including this one, ends with a project to make for yourself or as a gift.

Each chapter project and idea is marked to give you an approximation of the time required to complete it. Refer to the "Time Estimates" chart for an explanation of the rating system.

Time Estimates

These are general estimates of working times and presume you have familiarized yourself with the techniques and have the supplies purchased and ready.

⏲	One hour or less
⏲⏲	One to two hours
⏲⏲⏲	Allow an afternoon or evening
⏲⏲⏲⏲	Time varies – Allow one day
⏲⏲⏲⏲⏲	Some planning needed – Allow several days

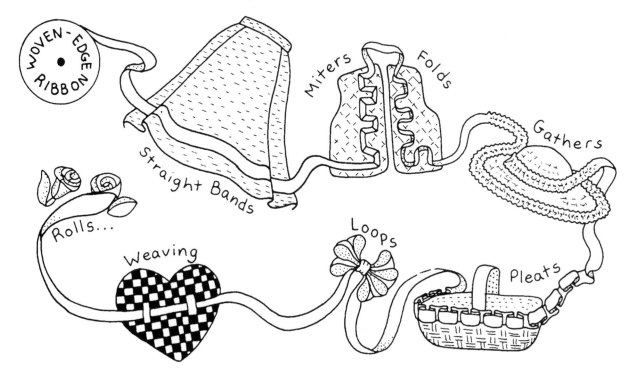

WOVEN-EDGE RIBBON

Straight Bands

Miters

Folds

Gathers

Rolls...

Weaving

Loops

Pleats

"I Love a Brocade" Ornament

I am enchanted by the beauty of brocade ribbons. I feel compelled to buy them, even when I have no special project in mind. I therefore tend to collect one-yard lengths of brocades I can't live without. To justify my purchases, I use them to make these little ornaments. They make intriguing package ties, hostess gifts, and party favors. For a special surprise, put a jingle bell inside.

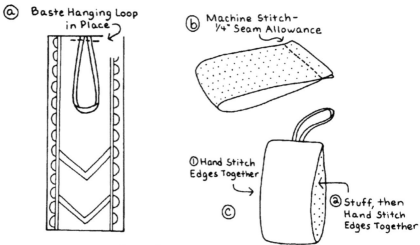

Fig. 1.16 Making the brocade ornament.

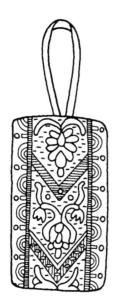

Fig. 1.15 "I Love a Brocade" Ornament.

Supplies:
6" of 1-1/2"-wide brocade (ornament)
5" of 1/16"-wide ribbon (hanging loop)
Polyester fiber stuffing
Sewing thread to blend with the brocade

a. Fold the 1/16" wide ribbon in half to make a loop. Place its ends even with one end of the brocade and on its top side.

b. Fold the brocade ribbon crosswise, right sides together. Machine stitch the ends together with a 1/4" seam allowance. Turn right sides out.

c. With sewing thread, stitch the left edges together. Fill the inside with a bit of polyester stuffing. Stitch the other edges together.

2. Creative Ribbon Borders

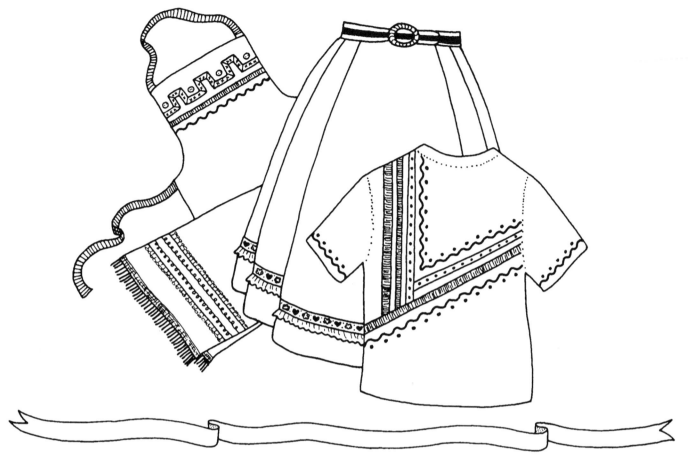

Border Basics

Trim hand- and ready-made items with a flourish using ribbon borders. Add borders to fabric creations such as aprons, towels, and skirts; apply them to baskets, jewelry boxes, and lampshades. This chapter introduces flat or two-dimensional border possibilities. Later chapters cover the three-dimensional border possibilities of gathers and pleats.

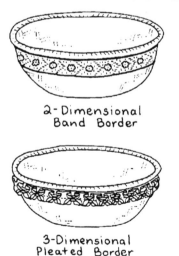

2-Dimensional
Band Border

3-Dimensional
Pleated Border

Fig. 2.1 *This chapter presents two-dimensional borders. Pleats and gathers, covered in later chapters, add a three-dimensional aspect.*

Place flat borders in a straight line or follow the perimeter of an object using turns made with folds and miters. (Figure 2.2.) Flat borders range from the simplicity of a plain band of ribbon, as shown in Figure 2.2, to elaborate combinations of ribbons, trims, and other embellishments, shown in Figure 2.3. Let your imagination soar!

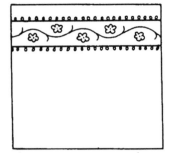

Straight Border

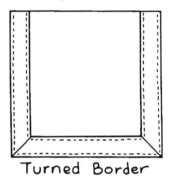

Turned Border

Fig. 2.2 *A flat border can lay in a straight line, or follow the perimeter of an object using miters and folds.*

Fig. 2.3 *Embellishments change borders from plain to fancy.*

As a rule of thumb, more intricately decorated borders show off best on plain foundations. Conversely, a plain ribbon provides good contrast to a busy foundation. For instance, apply a plain band of satin or grosgrain as a border to ease the transition between two different prints on a skirt. (Figure 2.4.)

Fig. 2.4 *Choose plain borders for busy backgrounds, and embellished borders for plain backgrounds.*

Applying a Flat Ribbon Border

Sewn Borders

Sew ribbon borders by hand or machine. Baste first to ensure accurate placement (see Pinning and Basting on page 8). On most ribbons, stitch just inside each edge with a matching or neutral thread. For hand sewing, use a blind stitch just inside the ribbon's edge, or a blind hem catching the edge. (Figure 2.5.) Watch the stitch tension to keep the ribbon flat, not puckered, at the edges. Stitching down the center is sometimes appropriate for narrow ribbons. Most times, however, I prefer to stitch both edges. Be sure to stitch both edges in the same direction to avoid distorting the ribbon. (Figure 2.6.)

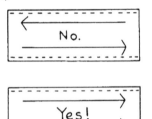

Fig. 2.6 *When machine stitching borders, stitch along both edges in the same direction.*

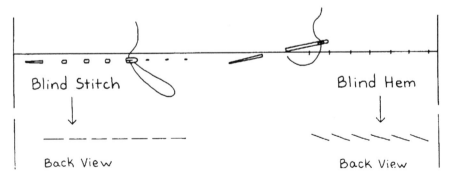

Fig. 2.5 *Use the blind stitch or blind hem to hand stitch ribbon in place.*

No-Sew Applications

Iron-on adhesives which hold without stitching are helpful when applying ribbon borders to fabric. They are especially useful for applying ribbon to stretch fabrics such as jersey. Figure 2.7 shows a T-shirt decorated with ribbon bands applied with iron-on adhesive. Before applying the

Fig. 2.7 Use washable, iron-on adhesives to embellish a T-shirt with bands of ribbon.

ribbon, I stretched the T-shirt on a cardboard T-shirt board (unwaxed side), such as that used for painting T-shirts. My shirt is decorated only on the front. I first turned the raw ends under and fused them, then I fused the ribbons to the shirt.

Borders can be applied to baskets, boxes, and such with white glue. Hot-melt glues are too thick and quick-drying to use with most flat borders, except for gluing the overlap of the ends.

Make a Sampler

Making samplers is a good way to practice basic techniques and to build models for reference. Two samplers are shown in this chapter—one of basic techniques for embellishing flat ribbon borders and using miters and folds (Figure 2.8), and one showing folded border variations (Figure 2.24 on page 20).

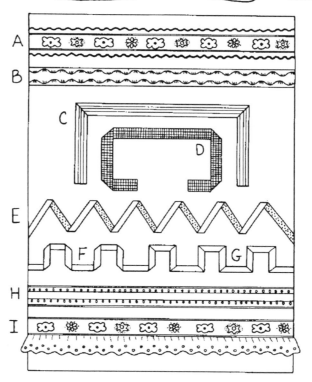

Fig. 2.8 Sampler of basic embellishments, miters, and folds.

Straight Ribbon Borders With a Special Touch

Adding embellishments transforms a ribbon border from ordinary to extraordinary. Here are four ways to add spice to straight band borders. The location of each on the sampler diagram in Figure 2.8, is shown in parentheses.

1. Add trims, such as rick rack or braid, above and below a jacquard-loomed ribbon. (Sampler Row A.) Tuck trims under ribbon edges as well. (See Figure 2.33 on page 23.)

Hand or machine embroidery can be used in the same way, above and below a ribbon.

2. Use decorative machine or hand embroidery stitches to sew a plain ribbon to a foundation fabric. (Sampler Row B.) For borders applied to baskets, decorate the ribbon before application.

3. Place a narrow ribbon on top of a wider one. A feather-edge satin on top of a plain-color grosgrain makes a lovely border. (Sampler Row H.)

4. Tuck an eyelet ruffle under one or both edges of a ribbon. (Sampler Row I.) These are available by the yard at fabric stores. Also use lace ruffles and pleated or gathered ribbon, making your own or using ready-made. Baste the trim in place while basting the edge of the ribbon.

Increasing Border Options Using Miters and Folds

Miters and folds free borders from the confines of following only a straight path. With these tools, a border can follow the perimeter of something such as a placemat. (Figure 2.9.) In addition,

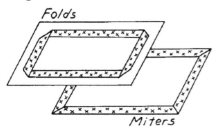

Fig. 2.9 *Miters and folds allow borders to follow the perimeter of an item such as a placemat.*

miters and folds open up a new range of interesting border variations to use alone or combined with some of the special touches discussed in the previous section. Folds are especially versatile, taking ribbon on intricate paths to create lively borders. Folds can also be used to create motifs—in essence, drawing with ribbon.

The Basics of Miters and Folds

Miters

Miters allow you to turn 90° corners and follow a squared edge. (Figure 2.8, Row C, on page 15; Figure 2.10.) Ribbons from 3/8" to 1" wide are easiest to miter. Since only one side of the ribbon will show, single-face ribbon is adequate, although double-face is fine too.

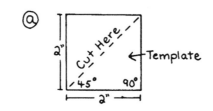

Fig. 2.10 *Miters follow a squared perimeter.*

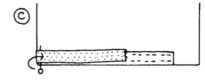

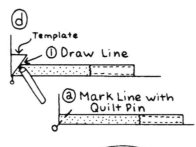

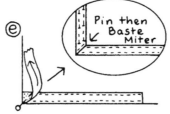

Fig. 2.11 *How to miter ribbon.*

When choosing patterned ribbons for miters, finger press a test miter before purchasing to see that it will produce a pleasing result. See if pattern motifs will look nice at the miters. This is especially important with prominent patterns, such as stripes, plaids, and gingham checks.

Making miters

With the following steps, perfect miters can be turned. Refer to Figure 2.11. The example of a placemat is used.

a. Make a cardboard or plastic template for a 45° angle by cutting out a perfect square, then marking and cutting along one of the diagonals.

b. Beginning along the bottom edge of the placemat, place the ribbon so one of its edges follows the bottom edge of the placemat. Pin both edges until you reach the corner. Pin up to the corner. Place a quilt pin crosswise at the corner, as shown. Baste ribbon edges.

c. Fold the long end of the ribbon back onto the pinned portion.

d. With the template, mark a 45° angle from the corner to the inside edge of the ribbon, as shown at "1". Move the pin along this line, as shown at "2".

e. Fold the loose end of the ribbon over the quilt pin and up toward the left side of the placemat. Pin and baste the mitered corner. Continue

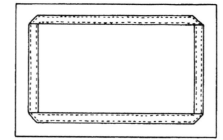

pinning, basting, and mitering all the way around the placemat.

Sewing miters

Miters can be stitched along both edges (Figure 2.12, top), or stitched only along the inside edge. (Figure 2.12, bottom.) For a crisply folded miter, lightly press the miter with a warm iron, or stitch a few blind stitches in the miter, going only through the ribbon, not the foundation fabric.

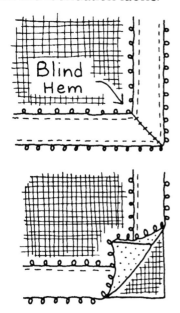

Fig. 2.12 Stitch mitered ribbon in place along both edges (top) or along only the inside edge (bottom). If needed, use a blind hem sewing only through the ribbon.

Folds

Folded corners lend an informal air to borders because they create "softer" corners. (Figure 2.8, Row D, on page 15.) Because folds do not create squared corners, they look best placed in from the edge. (Figure 2.13.) Folds require a double-face ribbon, such as grosgrain or taffeta, but the faces do not have to

Fig. 2.13 Folded ribbon creates informal, "soft" corners.

be identical. (See Figure 2.8, Row E, on page 15.)

Making folds

To fold a corner, simply turn the ribbon over or under itself when reaching a turning point. (Figure 2.14.) Whether the ribbon is folded over or under does not make a major difference visually unless the ribbon used has two different faces. In Figure 2.18 on page 19, compare the difference in effect between "A" and "B". Try both ways to see which is preferable for a particular ribbon.

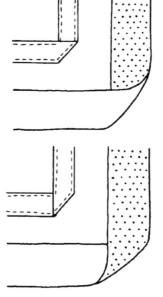

Fig. 2.14 To fold ribbon, turn the length forward or back upon reaching a turning point.

Sewing folds

There are two ways to sew folded corners. Sew around the inside and outside edges of the ribbon, including the folds. (Figure 2.15A.) Where stitching across the fold would interrupt the pattern on a ribbon, a lock-and-carry method can be used. (Figure 2.15B.)

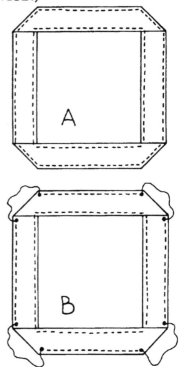

Fig. 2.15 To stitch folds: A. Stitch around the perimeter at each edge. B. Stitch the outside perimeter by stopping at each fold and carrying the thread across the fold. Stitch around the inside perimeter.

To lock-and-carry, stitch along the outer edge of the ribbon until a fold is reached. Set the stitch length at zero and take two or three stitches. Raise the presser foot and pull several inches of top thread through the needle. Move the work past the fold so the needle will go down at the other side of the fold. Put the top thread behind the presser

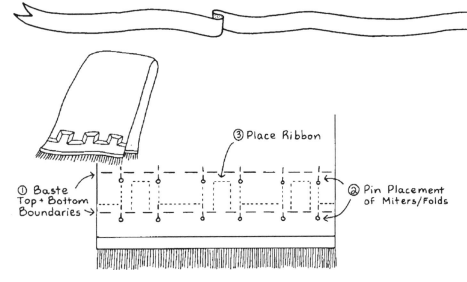

Fig. 2.16 *Pinning and basting assures accurately placed miters and folds.*

foot and lower the foot. Take two or three stitches at zero stitch length, then return to the regular stitch length and stitch to the next fold. In other words, don't stitch down the fold. Stitch the inner edge around its perimeter as usual. (Figure 2.15B.)

Creating Borders with Miters and Folds

Geometric borders can be created using repeated patterns of miters and folds. My favorite ribbon for these is 3/8"- or 5/8"-wide grosgrain. Try feather-edge satin, picot-edge taffeta and Jacquards as well.

Marking Geometric Borders

Careful marking of the foundation fabric ensures accurate placement of the motifs which make up the border. One alternative is to measure by eye, using a clear plastic ruler with a grid to help with placement.

Figure 2.16 shows a quick and accurate method for marking border motifs—in this example, on a towel.

1. Determine the top and bottom boundaries of the border. Baste these in place on the foundation fabric.

2. Using quilt pins and a clear plastic ruler, measure where each miter or fold should be placed and mark the fabric with quilt pins.

3. Pin the ribbon to the foundation following the basting and quilt pin markings. Step back and take a look—are the border motifs evenly placed? If so, baste the ribbon in place, then machine stitch.

You may also find water-soluble marking pens, pencils, or chalk helpful for marking the foundation fabric. Follow the manufacturer's instructions and test any marking device on a sample first.

Mitered Square Border

Miters can be used to make an elegant squared border pattern. (Figure 2.8, Row G, on page 15.) Use identical measurements lengthwise and crosswise on each square (Figure 2.17A), elongate the squares in either direction, or alternate two different size motifs. (Figure 2.17B.)

Sew both edges of these borders.

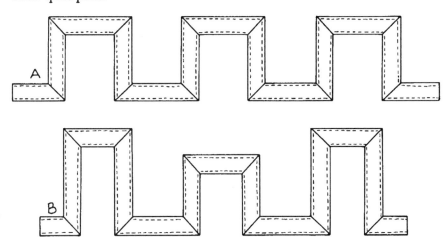

Fig. 2.17 *Mitered borders can have: A. Equal measurements for the motifs and the intervals between. B. Varied measurements for the motifs and intervals.*

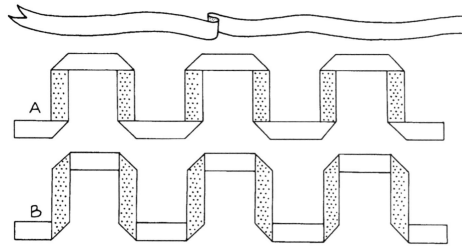

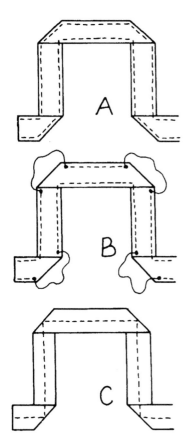

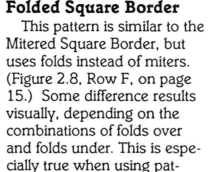

A

B

Fig. 2.18 Compare examples A and B, both using a ribbon with a one sided pattern. Note the slight difference in effect that occurs with different combinations of folds to the front and back.

Pointed Border

Folding ribbon into points creates a lively pattern. (Figure 2.8, Row E, on page 15.) Using ribbon that has polka dots on one face and is plain on the other creates an interesting combination. Try bending different angles for the points or overlapping two pointed borders. (Figure 2.20.) Use a point or two on a pocket to echo the point at the bottom of the pocket. (Figure 2.21.)

Folded Square Border

This pattern is similar to the Mitered Square Border, but uses folds instead of miters. (Figure 2.8, Row F, on page 15.) Some difference results visually, depending on the combinations of folds over and folds under. This is especially true when using patterned ribbon. (Figure 2.18.)

To sew a Folded Square Border, stitch around the perimeters (Figure 2.19A), use the lock-and-carry method (Figure 2.19B), or, if the ribbon is 3/8" wide or less, stitch in the center of the ribbon (Figure 2.19C).

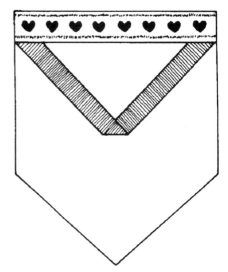

Fig. 2.21 Echo the bottom of a pointed pocket with a ribbon point decoration.

A

B

C

Fig. 2.19 To sew folded borders: A. Sew around each perimeter. B. Use the lock-and-carry method. C. Stitch down the center of narrow ribbons.

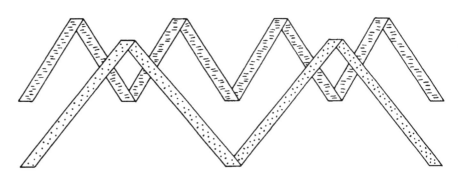

Fig. 2.20 Try different angles for points and even overlap two borders.

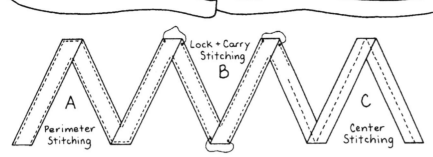

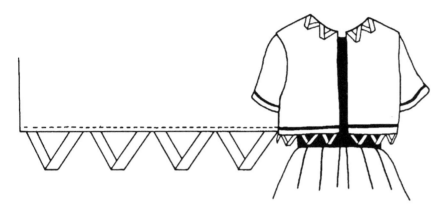

Fig. 2.22 To sew pointed borders: A. Sew around each perimeter. B. Use the lock-and-carry method. C. Stitch down the center of narrow ribbons.

Folded Border Variations

The sampler in Figure 2.24 shows just a few of the unique borders that can be created using folds.

1. Change the shape of motifs and the spacing between motifs. (Figure 2.24, Row A, B, C.)

2. Combine two borders. (Figure 2.24, Rows D, E, F.)

3. Add embellishments such as buttons, bows, rosebuds, other ribbons and trims, fabric paint, and embroidery. (Figure 2.24, Rows E, F.)

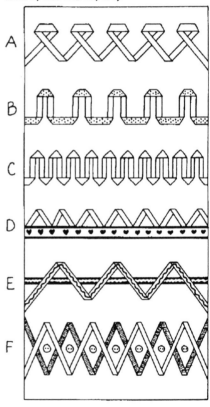

Fig. 2.23 Pointed edging: Use a pointed border extending beyond the edge of a garment for an interesting effect.

Stitch pointed borders around the perimeters (Figure 2.22A) or use the lock-and-carry method. (Figure 2.22B.) On narrow ribbons, it is sometimes suitable to stitch in the center. (Figure 2.22C.)

Pointed ribbon borders make an unusual edging for clothing or placemats, with the bottom points free of the foundation fabric. (Figure 2.23.) This edging can go in circles too. I used it in grosgrain ribbon to create the rays of the sun on a felt door decoration shown in the color photographs.

Fig. 2.24 Folded borders take on many forms from simple to intricate.

Drawing With Ribbon— Using Folds to Create Motifs

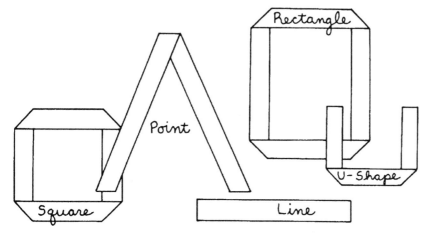

Fig. 2.25 Fold ribbon to create a variety of shapes, motifs, and letters.

Planning Motifs

1. Break down the desired motif into its basic shapes— points, lines, rectangles, squares, or U-shapes. (Figure 2.29.)

By combining folded shapes, such as squares, rectangles, lines, points, and U-shapes, ribbon becomes a drawing tool. (Figure 2.25.) Create arrows, spirals, letters, trees, flowers, houses, and other motifs from ribbon. A house with lace gingerbread under the roof (Figure 2.26) and a Christmas tree with a polka dot garland (Figure 2.27) are shown. A welcome sign is also shown. (Figure 2.28.)

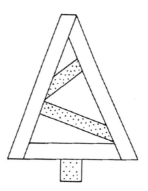

Fig. 2.27 A pine tree becomes a Christmas tree by adding a polka dot ribbon garland.

My favorite ribbon for "drawing" is 3/8"-wide grosgrain. It is double-face and easy to work with. My favorite foundation fabric is felt. It is substantial and easy to sew on.

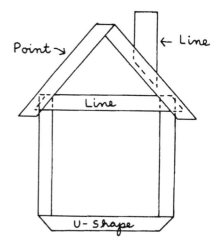

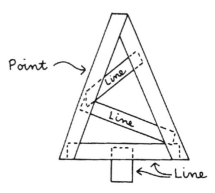

Fig. 2.29 To decide how to construct a motif, break it into basic shapes.

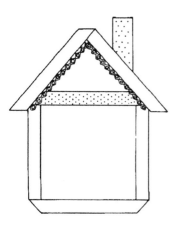

Fig. 2.26 House motif with lace edging under the eaves.

Fig. 2.28 Create signs using ribbon to form letters and punctuation. The bottom of the exclamation point is four short lengths of ribbon arranged in a circle and topped with a button.

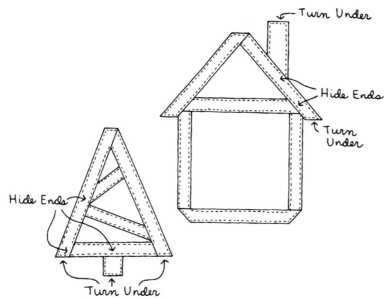

Fig. 2.30 *Determine where raw ends can be hidden under other ribbon lengths or where they must be turned under.*

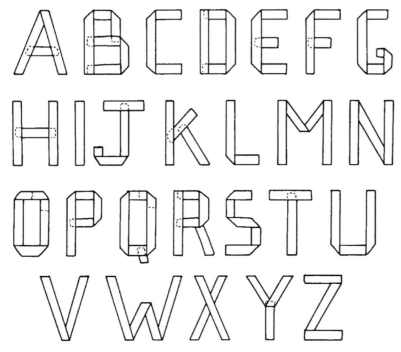

Fig. 2.31 *A ribbon alphabet. Dotted lines show where ribbon ends are tucked under other ribbon lengths.*

2. Determine where raw ends can be hidden or turned under to retard ravelling. (Figure 2.30.)

3. Determine how best to sew the motif. Usually stitching around the inside and outside perimeter is best. A center line of stitching may be adequate on simple shapes of very narrow ribbon. On motifs such as the house shown in Figure 2.30, which are made up of more than one shape, consider if one part of the picture must be placed and stitched before the others. For the house, I stitched the U-shape and top line before placing the roof and chimney. (See Figure 2.29.)

Making the Motifs

Rather than try to create a motif on the foundation fabric, develop it on the foam-board pin board first, then transfer it to the foundation fabric for basting and stitching. Graph paper pinned to the board is a great help in designing the motifs. Pin the layers of the folds together with pleat or silk pins, and use quilt pins to tack the motif to the pin board.

Rather than try to estimate the amount of ribbon a particular motif will require, fashion it from a long length, cutting the excess ribbon only as the motif becomes finalized.

Good Morning Placemats and Napkin-Ring Set ⏰⏰⏰

Make this pretty set in colors to match your breakfast area or china. The placemats have a built-in coaster for a coffee mug up to 3" in diameter. For larger mugs, re-measure the coaster area and adjust the ribbon and rick rack yardage.

Supplies

(For two placemats and rings)

5/8 yard medium-weight washable poly/cotton fabric for top of mats and for napkin rings (I used Weaver's K cloth)

1/2 yard poly/cotton broad-cloth for back of mats

5 yards 7/8"-wide washable ribbon (I used gingham check taffeta)

2 packages (2-1/2 yards each) medium rick rack

Fusible medium-weight interfacing sufficient for two strips, 2-1/2" x 5" each

Sewing thread to match ribbon and placemats

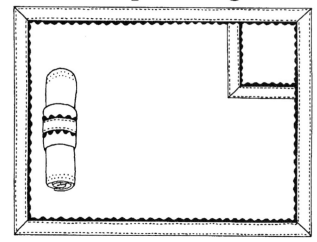

Fig. 2.32 *Make the Good Morning placemat and napkin-ring set bordered in a combination of ribbon and rick rack to complement your china. The placemat has a built-in coaster.*

Placemats:

Refer to Figure 2.33.

a. Preshrink all fabric, ribbon, and rick rack.

b. Cut a rectangle, 15" x 20", from the top material and from the backing material. With right sides together, using a 1/2" seam allowance, machine stitch each top piece to a backing piece. Leave a 5" opening in the middle of one 20" side. Clip corners and turn each mat right-side-out. Press

the mats flat, folding in the edges of the 5" opening. Baste the opening closed.

c. Pin, then baste, ribbon to the upper right corner of each mat to form the coaster, mitering the corner. While basting the inner edge of the ribbon, add rick rack so half of it is hidden under the ribbon to create a scalloped edge. Machine stitch just inside both edges of the ribbon, stitching in the same direction for each edge.

d. Starting at the "X" near the bottom left corner of the mat and following the directional arrow, pin, then baste, the ribbon to the edge of the placemat. Miter the corners and add rick rack to the inside edge of the ribbon as explained in Step c. When the ribbon returns to the starting point, turn the top raw end under 1/4" to finish. Machine stitch just inside both edges of the ribbon, stitching in the same direction for each edge.

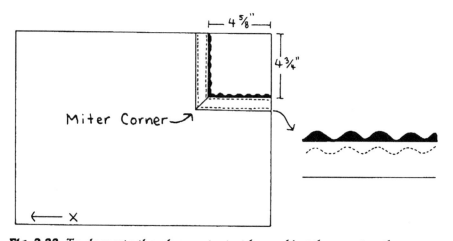

Fig. 2.33 *To decorate the placemat, start by making the coaster, then place the ribbon and rick rack around the perimeter of the mat, starting at the "X" and following the arrow.*

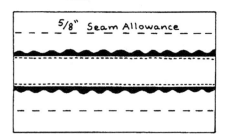

Napkin Rings:

Refer to Figures 2.34 and 2.35.

a. Cut 4 strips of placemat top material, 3-1/2" x 6", and 2 pieces fusible interfacing, 2-1/2" x 5".

b. Center the interfacing on the wrong side of two of the 3-1/2" x 6" strips. Fuse.

c. On the other two strips, pin, baste, and sew ribbon with rick rack inserted under each edge, as shown in Figure 2.34.

d. Place each decorated piece on an interfaced piece, right sides together. Stitch each 6" edge with a 5/8" seam allowance. Turn right side out and lightly press flat.

e. Turn in the raw edges 1/2". Machine stitch each end closed. With right sides facing out, bring the turned-in ends together to form a ring. Overcast the ends together. (Figure 2.35.)

Fig. 2.34 Decorate the napkin ring with a band of ribbon and rick rack in the center.

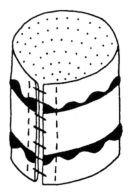

Fig. 2.35 Bring the ends of the napkin ring together and overcast.

3. Gathered Ribbon Ruffles

Ruffle Basics

Gathering is the process by which ribbon is pulled into tiny folds, or **gathers**, along a line of stitches, known as the **gathering line**. The end product of gathering is a **ruffle**. Dress up the neckline of a bodice, a pocket, or a hat with ruffles. Use them to trim a vest or basket. Ruffles are versatile because they gracefully go around curves when a flat length of ribbon can't.

Choosing Ribbon

Ribbon that is soft and supple gathers best. Single-face satin ribbon is ideal, as are silk and soft taffeta. These

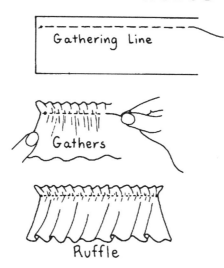

Fig. 3.1 *A line of stitches is pulled up into gathers. The gathered piece is called a ruffle.*

ribbons have a sheen that is enhanced by gathering. A sampler of delicate, silk ruffles is shown in the color photographs. When choosing a ribbon, check its suitability by taking up a few gathers with your fingers. Even some grosgrain, normally thought of as a heavier ribbon, gathers nicely.

When a narrow ribbon is needed and must be washable, seam binding is a perfect choice. Brands like Wright's Soft and Easy come in beautiful colors and have a subtle, woven-in pattern. Flat laces can be gathered as well.

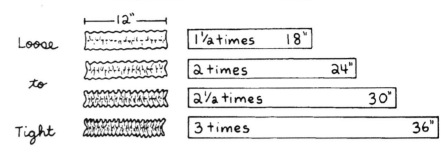

How Much Ribbon to Use

Gathering requires 1-1/2 to 6 times the finished length, depending on how tightly gathered you want the finished ruffle. Ruffles can range from loosely to tightly gathered. This depends on personal preference and the variety of ribbon.

Test your preference by making 6" to 12" sample ruffles. Figure 3.2 shows the amount of ribbon needed to make a 12" satin ruffle with loose to tight gathers. For 6" ruffles, divide the yardages in half. Very thin ribbons such as silk taffeta and seam binding are more easily pulled into very tight gathers using up to six times the finished length.

Be generous in estimating yardage. A good starting rule of thumb is to allow 2 to 2-1/2 times the finished length. Thus, if a 12" ruffle is needed, a minimum of 24" to 30" of ribbon would be required. I would, however, purchase at least 17" more to have sufficient ribbon to finish raw ends and make a 6" sample ruffle.

It is not always easy to determine the desired tightness, and thus the amount of yardage needed, before actually making a ruffle. I feel most comfortable starting with a length of ribbon longer than I could possibly need, which I gather until I have the right length ruffle of the desired tightness. This way, if I have miscalculated or decide I want a tighter ruffle, I can easily gather more ribbon. Figure 3.3 shows how to do this.

Fig. 3.2 *Use less ribbon for a loose ruffle, and more for a tight one.*

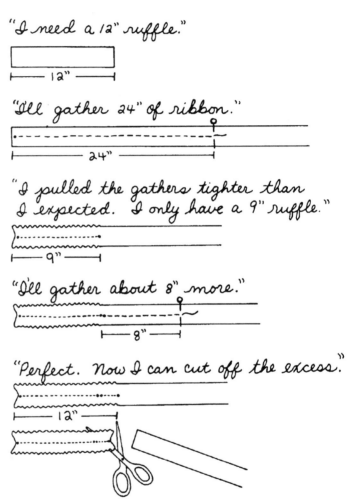

Fig. 3.3 *Rather than cut ribbon before gathering, work from a longer length so additional ribbon can be gathered until the ruffle is the right size.*

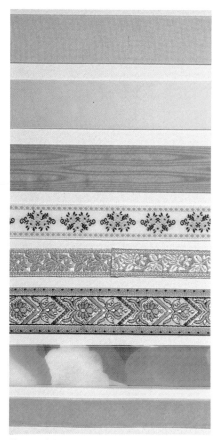

Basic ribbon varieties, *from top to bottom*, are grosgrain, satin, taffeta with moiré pattern, tapestry, Jacquard showing both faces, brocade, sheer, and velvet.

Decorate a scrap basket. Also shown are a color card of Japanese silk ribbons (*background*); polka-dot ribbon in satin, sheer and grosgrain (*foreground, left*); and "I Love a Brocade" ornaments (*foreground, right*).

Novelty ribbons, *from top to bottom*, are wrinkled, picot sheer, pearl-edge satin, cut satin, flower ribbon, ribbon and lace, taffeta with iridescent threads, and two metallics.

One-of-a-kind ribbons, *from top to bottom*, are embroidered grosgrain, grosgrain with lace edging, two grosgrains joined with satin stitch, satin with machine-embroidered edges, two widths of grosgrain combined, and grosgrain painted with fabric pens.

Edge treatments, *from top to bottom*, are feather-edge, picot-edge, crochet-edge, and a wire-edge tied bow.

Satin ruffles

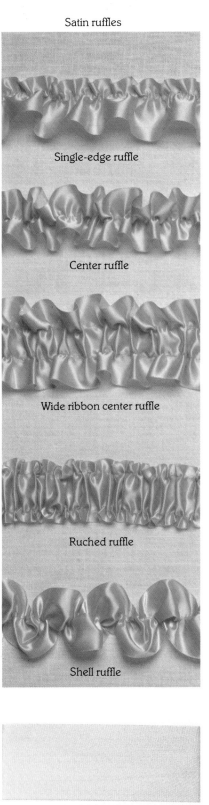

Single-edge ruffle

Center ruffle

Wide ribbon center ruffle

Ruched ruffle

Shell ruffle

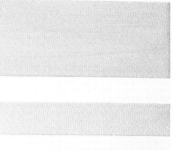

Embellished satin ruffles

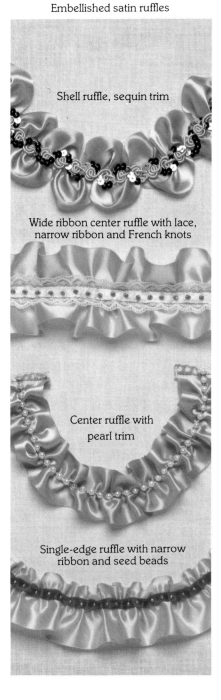

Shell ruffle, sequin trim

Wide ribbon center ruffle with lace, narrow ribbon and French knots

Center ruffle with pearl trim

Single-edge ruffle with narrow ribbon and seed beads

Silk ribbons (*left*) create delicate embellishments. *Above*, Tied bow (*top*), Rolled rose (*left*), and Spring Blossom (*right*). The silk ruffle sampler (*right*) uses ribbon widths of 32mm (1¼″), 13mm (⅜″), 7mm (¼″), 4mm (⅛″), and 2mm (1⁄16″).

Pleated grosgrain

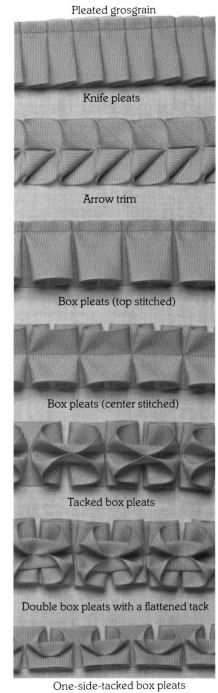

Knife pleats

Arrow trim

Box pleats (top stitched)

Box pleats (center stitched)

Tacked box pleats

Double box pleats with a flattened tack

One-side-tacked box pleats

Ribbons enhance a party mood: *clockwise from background center* are the 8½" round cake, bow angel, mini candy baskets with seam, binding ruffles, cake box, magic loop bow, satin napkin ring using a wide ribbon center ruffle, tulle rose with knotted ribbon streamers, flat ribbon rose on an eyelet rosette, and basket with a bow band border and a cluster of tiny roses.

At *left*, Christmas bell pull; *across the top*, part of a wire-edge garland. *Clockwise from top left* are Christmas wreath ornament, loop circle bow ornament, two camellias, bow tree (*inset*), mini rose bow ornament, Christmas tree mot in grosgrain, and two ribbon origami ornaments.

Ribbons sunny and bright: felt sun with pointed edging in grosgrain (*top right*), sunflower (*center*), knotted daisy (*bottom right*), hat with primrose cluster (*inset*), and the California poppy T-shirt (*background*).

At *center*, are a woven-ribbon greeting card and folded bow on a lace rosette. Around the outside are rose bows in four ribbons (*top*, grosgrain; *right*, wire-edge ombré taffeta; *bottom*, single-face satin; *left*, monofilament-edge sheet), and three flowers (*top left*, velvet rolled loop daisy; *top right*, striped moiré taffeta poppy with wire-edge ombré leaves; *bottom right*, knotted dahlia.)

Happy Valentines Day

Bow band border

Pump bow with tails

Two-color traditional bow

Pump bow

Double pump bow

Two-color tied bow

Double gathered bow

Quickie folded bow

Loop circle bow

Basket motif with pointed-edge weaving

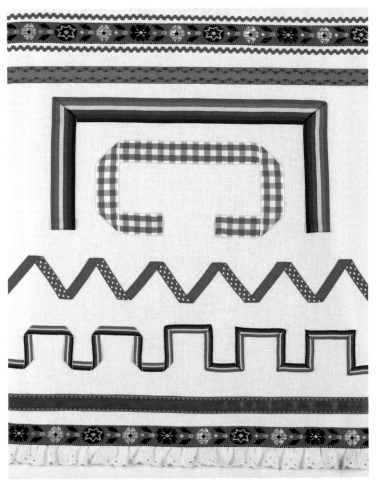

Ribbon borders, straight and turned. At *left*, sampler of folded border variations; at *right*, sampler of embellishments, miters, and folds.

Make breakfast a special time with the Good Morning Placemats and Napkin-Ring Set. The bowl contains a camellia of prepleated satin on a felt circle.

Ribbon colorful and playful. At *left*, folded house motif; at *right*, sweet peas with ribbon stems wrapped and tacked.

How to Gather Ribbon

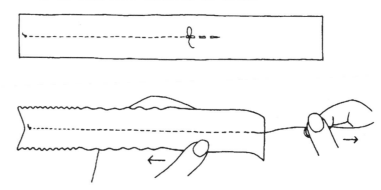

There are several ways to gather ribbon, depending on your preference and the kind of ribbon being used. With all methods, take care when pulling up the gathers to prevent the gathering thread from breaking. Move gathers along to the far end of the length of ribbon gently and a bit at a time rather than letting them bunch up along the way. This is especially important when gathering long lengths of ribbon or when gathering ribbons with substance, such as grosgrain.

Gather with polyester or cotton-covered polyester thread to further lessen the chance of breakage.

Gathering by Hand

To gather by hand, knot your thread and take a few back stitches into the ribbon to firmly lock the thread in place. Stitch a row of evenly spaced running stitches about 1/8" to 3/16" long. Pull up the stitches to gather and knot the other end. (Figure 3.4.) Experiment with different size stitches and spacings.

Machine Gathering

For long lengths of ruffles, gathering by machine is my preference. There are two ways to gather ribbon by machine—with a long stitch

Fig. 3.4 *To gather by hand, stitch a row of even running stitches and pull up the thread.*

length, or over cord. Check your machine's instruction manual for directions and hints which might modify the instructions which follow.

Long Stitch Gathering

This technique uses a long stitch length to sew a gathering line. The real secret to this technique is to relax the top thread tension just a bit to reduce the chances of thread breakage while pulling up the gathers. Practice will tell you how far to relax the tension on your machine. If relaxed too far, the gathers won't pull up nicely.

1. Place the ribbon face up under the presser foot. Using a medium stitch length and standard top tension, back stitch for a few stitches to lock the thread.

2. Relax the top thread tension a bit and change to the machine's longest stitch length. Stitch the gathering line and end by leaving a long thread tail. Do not lock the threads or backstitch.

3. Pulling on just the *bobbin* thread, gently pull up a few gathers. To prevent the gathering thread from breaking, move these gathers to the far end with the left fingers while the right fingers hold the thread tails and ribbon end. (Figure 3.5.) Continue in this manner until the ruffle is the

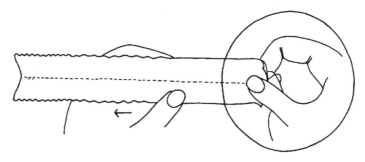

Fig. 3.5 *When machine gathering, hold the threads and ribbon end with the one hand while gently moving gathers along the length with the other.*

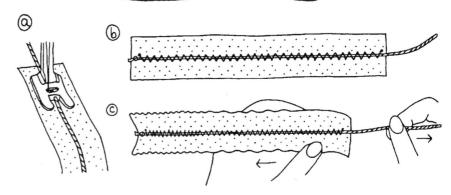

desired length. Knot the thread tails securely on the back of the ribbon and cut off the excess thread.

Gathering Over Cord

This method is especially recommended for long lengths and ribbons with substance to them, since the gathers pull up easily. With this method, a line of zigzag stitches is sewn over, but not through, a cord. Then the cord is drawn up through the zigzag tunnel.

A presser foot with a center hole to guide the cord as it feeds is almost essential. On some machines this foot may be called a cording or multi-cording foot. On my machine, the embroidery foot has such a hole. (Figure 3.6.) If you don't have one of these alternatives available, improvise by

Fig. 3.6 With cord gathering, a presser foot with a hole for the cord is essential. Left: Bernina Embroidery Foot. Right: Elna Multiple Cord Foot.

taping a piece of a soda straw to a standard presser foot.

A finer cord is needed for ribbon than might be used on fabric. If the cord is too heavy, the ribbon tends to fold in around the cord and never unfold again. Use heavy-duty quilting thread; fine cordonnet, such as DMC Cordonnet Special #50; or an equivalent. (Even a Pearl Cotton #8 is too heavy for most ribbon.)

Fig. 3.7 The Cord Gathering method: a. Zigzag stitch over cordonnet or other suitable cord. b. Knot one end of the cord with a substantial knot. c. Pull up the cord.

Ideally, the cord and sewing thread should match the ribbon color. Cord of neutral color can, however, be substituted.

Refer to Figure 3.7.

a. Thread cord through the hole in the presser foot from front to back, leaving a generous tail out the back.

Set the machine for zigzag stitch, using a medium stitch length and medium stitch width.

b. Stitch with the wrong side of the ribbon up, making sure the zigzag does not pierce the cord. Back stitch or knot the zigzag at both ends to lock the stitches.

c. At the beginning of the gathering line, securely anchor the cord in one of three ways—hand stitch the cord to the ribbon; make a *very large* knot in the cord; or wrap the cord in a figure 8 around a pin. Gather by pulling up the other end of the cord. Securely knot or hand stitch this other end of the cord.

Pulling Up a Ribbon Thread

Some ribbons can be gathered by pulling up a thread within the weave of the ribbon. The ribbon must be an even weave with no pattern, such as silk taffeta or some of the polyester taffetas. Because the ribbon threads are not intended to be used in this way, they are not strong enough to tolerate a lot of manipulation. Use this method only for very short lengths or where the ribbon is too narrow, such a 1/16"-wide silk, to gather any other way.

Secure the threads of one end by working white glue into the weave of the ribbon end, or, on a very narrow ribbon, tie a tight knot in the ribbon end. Make a small clip lengthwise in the other end of the ribbon, where the gathering line is to be. Isolate one

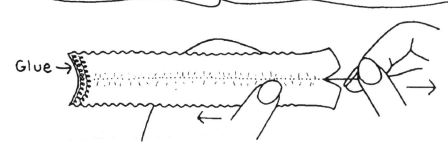

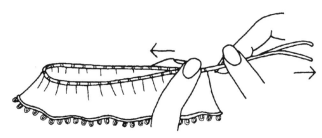

Fig. 3.8 To gather using a ribbon thread, work glue into one ribbon end. Make a clip in the other end, isolate a thread, and pull up.

Fig. 3.9 Simultaneously pull both ends of the picot-edge thread in one edge of a ribbon length.

may also be gathered in this manner.

Ribbon gathered this way has a tendency to create a circle, making impromptu flowers. (Figure 3.10.) Simply tie the thread ends together (or twist the wire ends) and sew a seam in the ribbon ends.

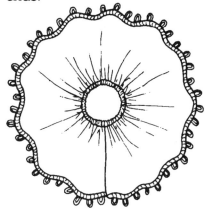

Fig. 3.10 When a picot thread is used to gather, the ribbon naturally curves into a circle. Sew the ends together for an impromptu flower.

lengthwise thread. Gently pull the isolated thread and pull up gathers. (Figure 3.8.)

The silk ribbons (except the blue shell ruffle) on the silk sampler in the color photographs were gathered using this method. I also used it with 1/16"-wide silk ribbon to make the hair for the Bow Angel in Chapter 5.

disappear as the thread is pulled. (Figure 3.9.) Once the gathering is complete, knot each thread end. Wire and monofilament edge ribbon

Pulling Up an Edge Thread

On picot-edge ribbons, the picot thread in one edge can be used as a gathering thread, creating a pretty ruffle which displays the other picot edge. This is not, however, true of feather-edge ribbon.

For this method, cut the length of ribbon to be gathered. At each end of the length, pull on the last picot loop to pull out the thread end. Pull up both thread ends to gather. The picots in the edge being gathered will

Kinds of Ruffles

Making a Sampler

Depending on the placement of the gathering line, different ruffles are created. Make a sampler of the various ruffles. Except for the Wide Ribbon Center Ruffle which requires wider ribbon, use 1-1/2"-wide single-face satin ribbon to practice with.

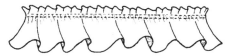

Fig. 3.11 Single-edge ruffle.

Single Edge Ruffle

Gathering along one edge is most often used when that edge will be sewn under fabric. (Figure 3.12.) Use a looser ruffle to reduce bulk.

Gathering 1/4" or more in from the edge makes a small ruffle above the stitching line as well as below. This is

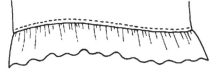

Fig. 3.12 Loosely gather along one edge for a ruffle to sew under a foundation fabric.

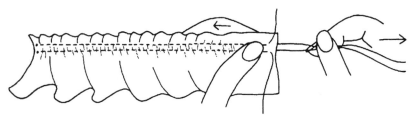

Fig. 3.13 *When two rows of gathering stitches are used, pull up both at the same time to keep them even.*

Fig. 3.14 *Add ruffles to pockets for a feminine touch.*

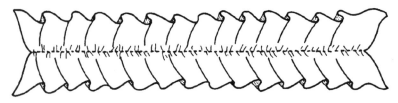

Fig. 3.15 *Center ruffle.*

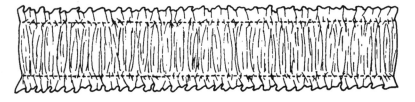

Fig. 3.16 *Ruched ruffles have both edges gathered.*

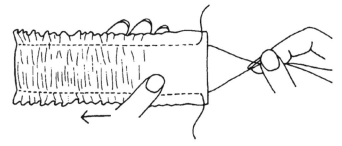

Fig. 3.17 *Keep the gathers in a ruched ruffle even by pulling up the threads at both edges simultaneously.*

especially attractive where the ruffle will be applied on top of other fabric. Using two rows of stitching rather than one makes a prettier ruffle for top application. Space the two rows 1/8" apart. For a 1/4" top ruffle, stitch the first line 1/4" in from the edge, and the second line 3/8" in from the

edge. Remember to stitch both in the same direction. Pull up both gathering threads simultaneously so the gathers stay even along the length. (Figure 3.13.)

Adding a ruffle to a pocket adds interest and a feminine touch to any garment, even a pair of jeans. Figure 3.14 illustrates three different ruffle placements for patch pockets.

Center Ruffle

Gathering ribbon down the center makes a lovely ruffle for top application. To center gather, lightly press a lengthwise fold in the ribbon to create a guideline, or use guides available on your sewing machine.

A Center Ruffle is a good choice where a very tightly gathered trim is needed. It is easily shaped into patterns.

For a pretty variation, stitch two gathering lines, one a bit above center and the other a bit below. Pull the gathers up simultaneously.

Ruched Ruffle

Gathering both edges is known as Ruching. When stitching by machine, be sure to stitch both gathering lines in the same direction. Draw up both gathering threads at the same time so the gathers stay even along both edges.

Use ruching to create ribbon straps for camisoles, nighties, and dresses.

Wide Ribbon Center Ruffle

A versatile ruffle is created in wide ribbon by stitching two rows of gathering near the center of the ribbon. On 2-1/4" wide ribbon, stitch a gathering line 3/4" in from each edge. Pull up the two gathering threads simultaneously for even gathers. (See Figure 3.17.) The end result is a ruffle with a ruched center and two edge ruffles. This is a pretty ruffle for a wide hat band or basket band. It also makes lovely napkin rings with both gathering lines decorated with trim. One is shown in the color photographs.

Shell Ruffle

This elegant ruffle looks exquisite in satin or moiré taffeta. It is very adaptable, as it can be shaped and will turn corners with ease. It is a perfect edging for a sun hat or vest. Shell Ruffles are the basis for several of the flowers in Chapter 6. Refer to Figure 3.20.

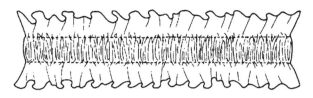

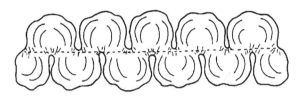

Fig. 3.18 *Wide ribbon center ruffle.*

Fig. 3.19 *Shell ruffle.*

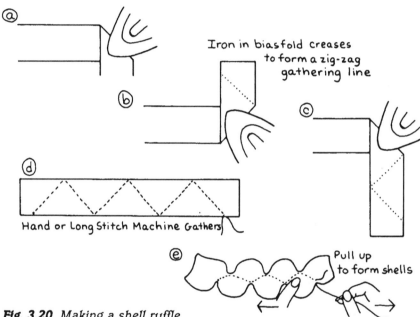

Iron in bias fold creases to form a zig-zag gathering line

Hand or Long Stitch Machine Gathers

Pull up to form shells

Fig. 3.20 *Making a shell ruffle.*

a. Leaving a sufficient raw end to be finished later, fold the top edge of the right ribbon end down on the bias, as shown. Press with a warm iron to crease a well-defined stitching guideline.

b. Open out the ribbon. At the point where the crease meets the top edge, fold the bottom edge of the right ribbon end up on the bias, as shown. Press a crease with the iron.

c. Continue alternating up and down bias folds, always manipulating the right end of the ribbon up or down each time. Pressing each fold creates a zigzag line across the entire length.

d. Use long stitch machine gathering to stitch along the zigzag line. (The cording method is difficult to use, since it is tricky to turn at each edge without catching the cord in the stitching.)

e. Carefully pull up the gathering thread. As it is pulled, the thread will center itself and little scallops will align themselves alternately above and below the gathering line. The scallops should puff out a bit to look like shells.

When making a Shell Ruffle on very narrow ribbon or seam binding, stitch the gathering line by hand.

Working With Ruffles

Taming Ruffles

Lengths of gathered ribbon sometimes twist as the gathers are pulled up. The ribbon can also fold in around the gathering line. Don't despair. Once the length is fully gathered, gently pull the edges apart where they have folded in, then pin the ruffle to the foam-board pin board and use fingers or the point of a quilt pin to coax the twists out of the ruffles. (Figure 3.21.) Even up the gathers along the gathering line at this time also.

It is sometimes frustrating to tame a tightly gathered center ruffle because it is hard to tell the two sides apart among the twists. Use two different colors or shades of thread as the top and bottom thread to differentiate them.

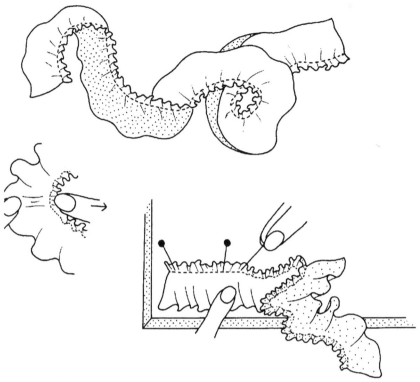

Fig. 3.21 *Tame ruffles by gently pulling on the edges, then pinning the ruffle to a pin board as it is straightened out. Use a quilt pin to help even up the gathers.*

Applying Ruffles

For a ruffle placed *on top of a foundation fabric,* I prefer to stitch it in place by hand, using a blind stitch. Stitching by machine tends to flatten the ruffle. In addition, when sewing by hand I can make last-minute adjustments to even up the ruffles as I sew.

When a ruffle is applied *under a foundation fabric,* I use the machine. I gather the ruffle using two gathering rows, then machine stitch it under the foundation so that my line of stitching falls between the two gathering rows.

Shell Ruffles are best applied with hand stitching. The little shells lose their liveliness under the pressure of machine stitching.

For craft projects, I prefer white glue to attach ruffles.

Embellishing Ruffles

Add a special finish to ruffles by embellishing the gathering line. A sampler of some embellishments is shown in the color photographs.

For best results in embellishing ruffles, use a ruffle with medium to loose gathers, and use two lines of gathers. Embellishments placed over such a ruffle will lie in place better.

Figure 3.22 illustrates where

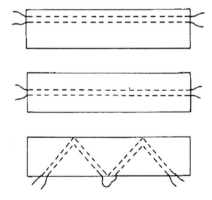

Fig. 3.22 *Use two gathering lines for embellished ruffles.*

to sew the two gathering lines for a ribbon to be embellished with a trim on top. Place the two gathering rows so they will be hidden under the trim. Note that two rows can be used for Shell Ruffles as well.

Christmas Wreath Ornament ⏰

By using the Cord Gathering method with wire instead of cord, a finished ruffle can be shaped into a circle. Use very thin (28-gauge) brass or floral wire, available at craft and hardware stores. Check your sewing machine's instruction manual to be sure this technique is compatible with your machine.

Supplies
24" of green seam binding
   (5/8"-wide satin ribbon
   may be substituted)
24" of 28-gauge brass or
   floral wire
Seam sealant
Small decorations such as
   beads and bows
Gold embroidery thread
   (hanging loop)

1. Treat the ends of the seam binding or ribbon with seam sealant.

2. Using the Cord Gathering method with wire instead of cord, stitch a line of gathers down the center of the seam binding or ribbon.

3. Push the gathers down the wire so you can cut the wire at about 4". Hold both ends of the wire together and twist

them to create a 2-1/4" diameter circle of ruffles. (Figure 3.24.) Cut off the excess wire with all-purpose shears (not your good scissors).

4. Hide the join with a tiny Tied Bow. (See page 49.) Sew tiny beads around the wreath for decoration. Add a gold loop to the top of the wreath to hang it.

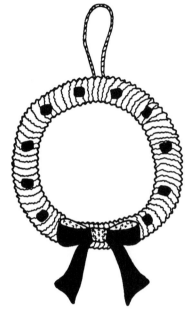

Fig. 3.23 Use wire in place of cord to make a Christmas wreath ornament from seam binding or ribbon.

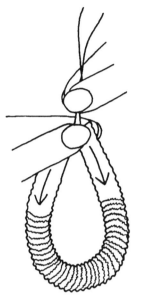

Fig. 3.24 To make the wreath, push the gathers to the center of the wire from both ends.

Heart Sachet ♡♡♡

Supplies

1 yard of 1-1/2"-wide single-face satin or moiré taffeta, medium to deep pink

5" of 3-1/2"-wide single-face satin, light pink

8" of 1/8"-wide satin, either shade of pink (optional hanging loop)

6" x 10" piece of white felt

Sewing thread to match the 1-1/2"-wide ribbon and the felt

A few tablespoons of rose scent potpourri or fragrant rose petals (available at craft stores)

White glue

Polyester fiber stuffing

Buttons, beads, tiny roses, bows, or other trims.

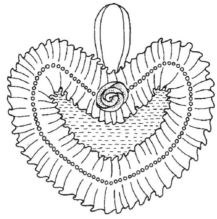

Fig. 3.25 The Heart Sachet is covered with satin ribbon and decorated with a taffeta ruffle and pearl trim. A silk rosebud adds a graceful finish.

1. Cut out two felt hearts, using the pattern in Figure 3.26.

2. Lay the 3-1/2" wide ribbon across one felt heart as shown by the dotted line on the pattern in Figure 3.26. Cut this ribbon to fit the sides and top notch of the heart. Run a small bead of white glue along the raw cuts in the ribbon to keep them from fraying. Lay the ribbon piece aside to dry.

3. With right sides facing out, machine stitch the two hearts together 1/4" in from the edge, sewing all the way around.

4. Carefully make a slit in one of the hearts as shown on the pattern in Figure 3.26. Loosely fill the heart with potpourri and polyester stuffing. Slip stitch the slit closed with white thread. Do not pull the stitches tight. The slit should lie flat.

5. Place the 3-1/2"-wide piece of ribbon over the heart with the slit. Slip stitch it to the heart, stitching around the heart's perimeter. Don't let your stitches go through to the other heart.

6. Center gather the 36" length of 1-1/2" wide ribbon. Pull up to make a 15" ruffle. Knot all threads on the wrong side.

Turn the raw ends under 1/4" twice to the wrong side and stitch with a blind hem.

7. For a hanging sachet, fold the 1/8"-wide ribbon in half and tack both ends to the top of the heart at the "X" on the pattern in Figure 3.26.

8. With the satin covered heart facing up, begin at the "X" in Figure 3.26, and place the ruffle around the outside of the heart. Place the ruffle so its outside edge extends a bit over the outside edge of the heart. Pin the ruffle in place so the gathers are evenly placed and the ends overlap at the top.

9. Blind stitch the ruffle in place with matching thread. Catch only the top heart—the stitches should not show on the back heart.

10. Add embellishments as desired to the top of the heart and the center of the ruffle.

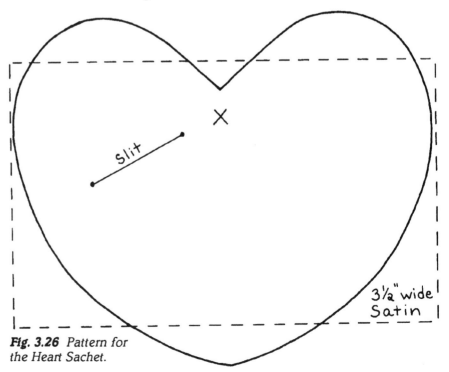

slit

✕

3½" wide Satin

Fig. 3.26 Pattern for the Heart Sachet.

4. Pleated Ribbon

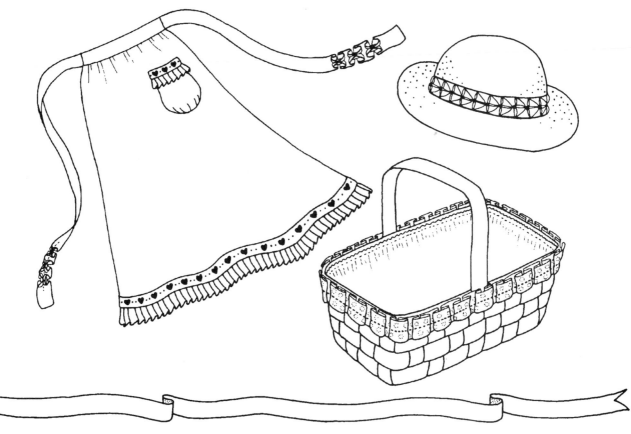

Pleat Basics

Making uniform folds in ribbon produces pleats. Pleating takes full advantage of the suppleness of woven-edge ribbon. Pleats add a dimensional flair to baskets, hemlines and pockets. As we will see in this chapter, pleats can also stand alone—to become a garland, ornament, or bell pull.

There are two basic pleats—**Knife** pleats and **Box** pleats. (Figure 4.1.) Pleats can be flat or they can have their edges tacked in various ways for extra dimensionality. Pleats left unpressed have a casual

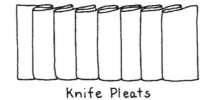

Knife Pleats

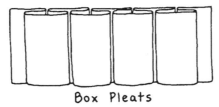

Box Pleats

Fig. 4.1 *There are two kinds of pleats—Knife and Box.*

softness. Pressed pleats have a crisp formality. Which to use is a matter of personal preference.

Choosing Ribbon

Use ribbons with some substance, such as grosgrain or satin. Grosgrain is the best ribbon to start with as it has a nice substance, pretty sheen, and is less slippery to work with than satin. Brocade and velvet usually are too substantial to pleat successfully. Single-face ribbon is sufficient for flat pleats. Tacked pleats often benefit from a double-face ribbon.

Pleat Anatomy

Figure 4.2A illustrates the parts of a pleat. Pleats have width and depth. **Pleat width** is the width of the visible surface of a pleat, and **pleat depth** is the measurement from the backfold to the placement line. (Figure 4.2B.)

In a **full depth** pleat, there is twice as much material behind the front, visible surface of the pleat as there is on the pleat front. So, a 1" knife pleat has a 1" depth and 2" in the underfold area. A 2" box pleat has a pleat depth of 1", and 4" total in the underfolds. (Figure 4.2C.) This takes more yardage, obviously.

A **shallow** pleat, however, has less depth in the underfold area. For instance, a 1" knife pleat might have just 1/2" in the underfold area, or a 2" box pleat might have just 1" in each underfold area. (Figure 4.2D.) Shallow pleats use less yardage and are helpful where a band of pleats with less bulk is required. A shallow pleat, however, loses some of the dimensionality that makes full pleats so pretty.

The instructions and measurements given in this chapter are for full pleats.

Measuring Pleats

Measuring ensures pleats will have uniform width and depth along the entire band of ribbon. There are several ways to do this.

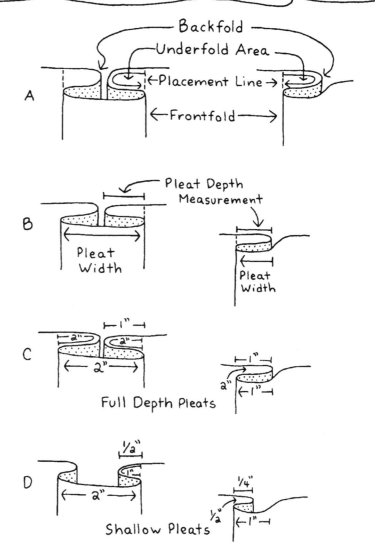

Fig. 4.2 A. Each part of a pleat has a special name. B. Measurements for pleat width and depth are commonly used. C. Full pleats have deep underfold areas. D. Shallow pleats have less depth in the underfold area.

Measure by Eye

Some people are able to measure well by eye. To check measurements, use a clear plastic ruler with a grid. (Figure 4.3.)

Measure With Gauges

Measuring with gauges is an old technique that produces accurate, uniform pleats. The gauges, made of cardboard, are used to help make pleat folds of the appropriate depth.

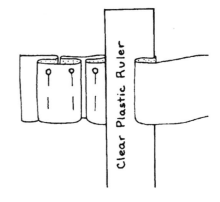

Fig. 4.3 A transparent plastic ruler with grid helps check the pleat depth on pleats made by eye.

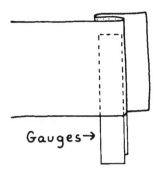

Gauges→

Fig. 4.4 Measuring with gauges is a quick way to create uniform pleats.

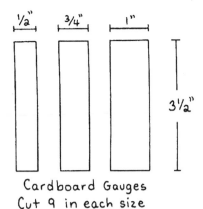

½" ¾" 1"

3½"

Cardboard Gauges
Cut 9 in each size

Fig. 4.5 Make cardboard gauges 3-1/2" long. Make sets of gauges 1/2" wide, 3/4" wide, and 1" wide, with 9 gauges per set.

(Figure 4.4.) Diagrams in the later sections on Knife and Box pleats show how to use them for each type of pleat. Don't let the diagrams scare you away from this technique. It is not hard and produces beautiful pleats. I have updated the technique to use the foam-board pin board and this makes it even easier. With practice, I have found it is quicker to make pleats by gauge than by eye. Pleats made with gauges can be pressed during the measuring process or left unpressed.

Making gauges

Cut sets of gauges from thin cardboard. Cut carefully so all gauges within a set are the same size. Make three sets— 1/2" wide, 3/4" wide, and 1" wide. Cut nine identical gauges for each set. Make all gauges 3-1/2" long so they will be longer than the ribbon to be pleated. (Figure 4.5.)

Measure with the Perfect Pleater

Make pressed Knife pleats with a tool called the Perfect Pleater by Clotilde. (See Sources of Supply on page 87.) Tuck ribbon into the folds

of the pleater's surface using your fingers or a plastic card, then press the pleats. (Figure 4.6.) Make pleats in various widths by skipping slats. They can range in width from 1/4" on up. All the pleats will have a depth of 1/4". The Perfect Pleater comes with complete instructions and handy tips.

Holding Pleats

Once pleats are measured, hold them in place with pleat, silk, or quilt pins; then baste them. Also helpful, especially when pleating by eye, are hair curl clips. They hold securely, but allow pleats to be easily adjusted. (See Figures 1.12 and 1.13.)

Basting pleats is essential. Baste near, but not directly over, the final stitching line. Use shorter stitches than for other purposes so the stitches securely hold each fold of the pleats. Care at this step pays off since ribbon pleats want to slip around when they are stitched on the machine.

Stitching Pleats

Machine stitching is easiest and most secure. Knife pleats are most commonly stitched along one edge. Box pleats are

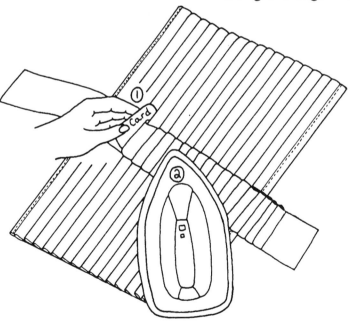

Fig. 4.6 The Perfect Pleater by Clotilde is handy for making pressed knife pleats. Tuck the ribbon into the folds of the Pleater with a plastic card (1) and press the pleats (2).

stitched along one edge or through the center. (Figure 4.7.) Where pleats will be tacked (see below), center stitching is used.

A well-basted band of pleats can be stitched directly to foundation fabric—stitched either under the edge of the foundation, or on top (Figure 4.8.). A band of pleats can also be stitched separately, then attached to a foundation.

Apply a band of pleats to non-sewable items such as baskets with white glue.

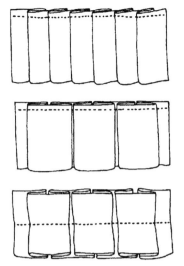

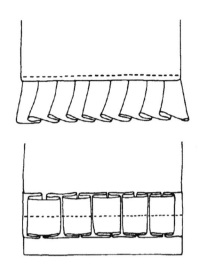

Fig. 4.7 Knife pleats are most commonly stitched at one edge. Box pleats are stitched at one edge or in the center.

Fig. 4.8 Stitch pleats under a foundation or on top.

Kinds of Pleats

Making a Sampler

Build your pleating skills by making a sampler of the various techniques in this chapter.

Make a band sampler to practice each technique along one length of ribbon. (Figure 4.9.) Purchase 3-1/2 yards of your favorite color 1-1/2"-wide grosgrain ribbon. Turn under the raw ends of the ribbon then make five pleats of each type—knife pleats, edge-stitched box pleats, center-stitched box pleats, and double box pleats. Leave about 3" between each set of pleats. On the center-stitched box and double-box pleats, tack two or three pleats to show this effect.

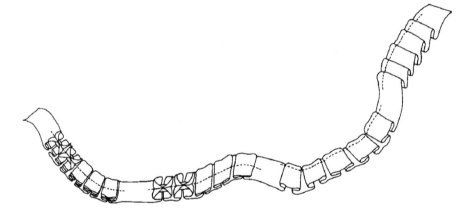

Fig. 4.9 Make a band sampler containing examples of various pleats along the ribbon length.

Shown in the color photographs is a traditional sampler of pleated ribbon bands displaying all of the techniques included in the chapter. Grosgrain ribbon 1-1/2" wide is a good choice to practice pleats.

Knife Pleats

Knife pleats all face in the same direction. Design them wide or narrow depending on the look desired. (Figure 4.11.) Knife pleats 1/2" wide are lovely in 1-1/2"-wide ribbon.

For knife pleats, use ribbon three times the finished length.

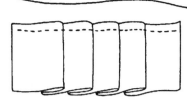

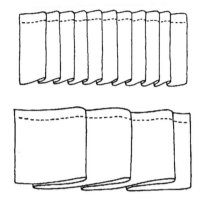

Fig. 4.10 *Knife pleats.*

Fig. 4.11 *Make narrow or wide knife pleats.*

Making Knife Pleats

Knife pleats by eye

To make knife pleats by eye, make an "S" curve in the ribbon by holding it in both hands and bringing one hand over the other to form an "S". (Figure 4.12.) Press this flat with your fingers to make the desired width pleat. Pin, then baste.

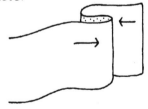

Fig. 4.12 *To make a knife pleat by eye, make an "S" curve in the ribbon and finger press it flat.*

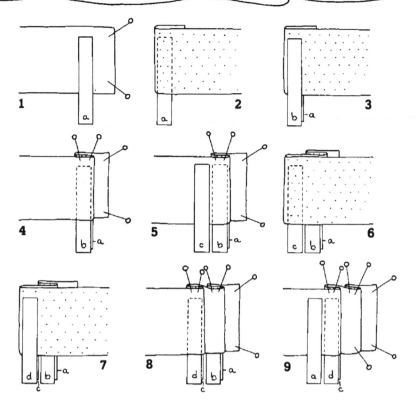

Fig. 4.13 *Using gauges and a pin board, knife pleats can be made quickly and accurately.*

Knife pleats by the gauge method

Use four 1/2" gauges. Refer to Figure 4.13.

1. Pin the righthand end of the ribbon length to the foam-board pin board. Leave at least 1" at the secured end. Lay one gauge, "a", on the ribbon with the top of the gauge about 1/4" below the top of the ribbon.

2. Hold gauge "a" in place while folding the long length of ribbon to the right over gauge "a".

3. Lay a second gauge, "b", on the ribbon directly over gauge "a".

4. Fold the long length of ribbon back to the left over gauge "b". With quilt pins, tack the top of the pleat to the pin board. Do not remove the gauges. Leaving them in place assures the next pleat will be placed accurately.

5. Place gauge "c" on the ribbon just to the left of the completed pleat.

6. Fold the long length of ribbon to the right over gauge "c".

7. Place gauge "d" on the ribbon directly over gauge "c".

8. Fold the long length of ribbon to the left over gauge "d". Tack the top of the pleat to the pin board as with the previous pleat.

9. Remove gauges "a" and "b". Tack the bottom of the first pleat to the pin board. Hold gauges "c" and "d" in place while making the next pleat.

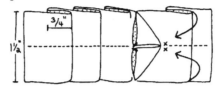

Repeat all the steps until the entire length of ribbon is pleated. Periodically, baste the pleats and remove excess pins. Move the basted ribbon length off the pin board as needed, keeping at least one completed pleat tacked to the board to ensure uniform placement of succeeding pleats. (Figure 4.14.)

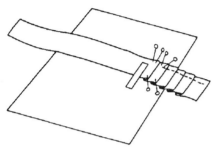

Fig. 4.14 Move basted lengths of pleating off the pin board, keeping one or two pleats on the board for reference.

Knife Pleat Variation

Arrow Trim

Decorate a basket, hat, or Christmas stocking with a band of Arrow Trim.

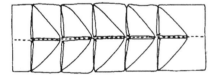

Fig. 4.15 Arrow Trim.

Arrow Trim begins with a band of full knife pleats with a pleat width that is half the width of the ribbon. For example, on a 1-1/2"-wide ribbon, the pleat width should be 3/4". Machine stitch the band of pleats in the center rather than at the top edge. Fold the top corner of the

frontfold of each pleat to the center. Hand tack it in place with two or three small stitches into the fold. Fold the bottom corner of the frontfold to the center and tack it in place with small stitches. Let

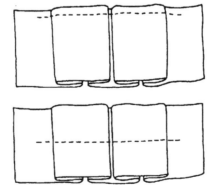

Fig. 4.16 Make Arrow Trim by center stitching knife pleats, then tacking the top and bottom edges of each frontfold to the center. Give the pleats a width one half the ribbon width.

the tacking thread travel to the next pleat on the back of the ribbon band or within the underfold area of the pleats.

Box Pleats

Box pleats result when two knife pleats face in opposite directions. One-inch-wide box pleats are nicely proportioned for 1-1/2"-wide ribbon.

Fig. 4.17 Box pleats—edge- and center-stitched.

Ribbon three times the finished length is required for box pleats.

Making Box Pleats

Box pleats by eye

To make box pleats by eye, form a knife pleat in one direction, then form one next to it but facing in the opposite direction. (Figure 4.18.)

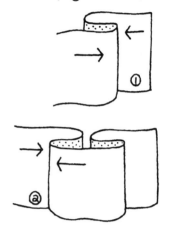

Fig. 4.18 To make a box pleat by eye, make a knife pleat in one direction (1), then make one facing the other direction (2).

Box pleats by the gauge method

Use five 1/2" gauges. Refer to Figure 4.19. This sounds more complicated than it is to do. You may find it helpful to mark each gauge alphabetically from a to e.

1. Tack the righthand end of the ribbon to the foam-board pin board. Leaving at least 1" at this end, make a knife pleat, as in Steps 1 – 4 of Figure 4.13.

2. Hold gauges "a" and "b" in place. Place gauge "c" on top of the ribbon, directly over gauges "a" and "b".

3. Fold the long length of ribbon to the right over gauge "c".

4. Place gauge "d" on top of the ribbon directly over gauge "c".

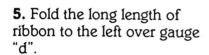

5. Fold the long length of ribbon to the left over gauge "d".

6. Place gauge "e" on the ribbon directly over the four below it.

7. Turn the frontfold of the top knife pleat to the left, letting gauge "c" fall away.

8. Remove gauges "a" and "b". Tack the right side of the box pleat to the pin board with quilt pins at the top and bottom. Tack the top left side of the pleat to the board but *do not* remove gauges "d" or "e".

9. Holding gauges "d" and "e" in place, begin the next pleat, using gauges "a" and "b". Once they are in place, remove gauges "d" and "e" and tack the bottom left side of the first pleat to the pin board.

Repeat all the steps until the entire length of ribbon is pleated. Move the basted

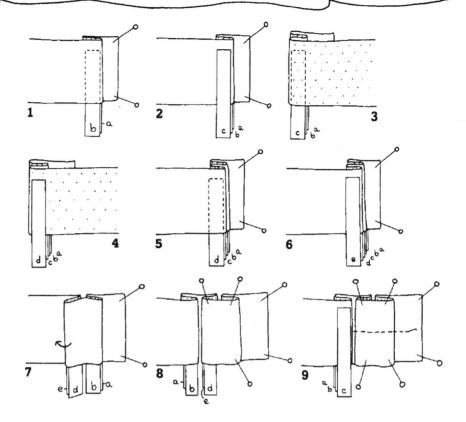

Fig. 4.19 *Make even box pleats quickly using gauges.*

ribbon length off the pin board as needed, keeping at least one completed pleat tacked to

the board to ensure uniform placement of the next pleats. (See Figure 4.14 on page 40.)

IDEA

Wire-Edge Ribbon Garland

Create a festive garland to decorate a doorway or mantle for Christmas, birthdays, or any special occasion

by making box pleats in wire-edge ribbon. Wire-edge ribbon is a joy to pleat because the pleats stay in place so well during the construction process. Have the pleats in groups with spaces between and decorate the spaces with

gold buttons, jingle bells, or other fanciful embellishments.

The red garland shown in the color photographs is a soft taffeta with gold trim. The garland is decorated with small, gold snowflakes.

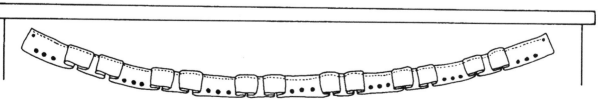

Fig. 4.20 *Make a garland in wire-edge ribbon, spacing groups of pleats at intervals and adding decorations in the intervals.*

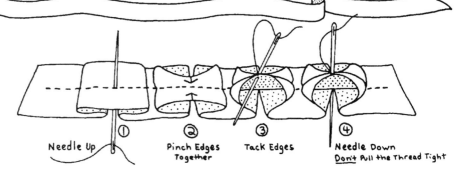

Box Pleat Variations—Enhancing the 3-D Effect

Tacked box pleats

To give center-stitched box pleats maximum dimensionality, bring the edges together at the center and hand tack them. The result is an intricate-looking and elegant pleat. Since the tacking thread will be visible at the edge of the ribbon, use a matching color.

Fig. 4.22 To tack box pleats: 1. Bring a needle up in the center of the pleat. 2. Pinch the edges of the pleat together. 3. Hold the edges together with 2 or 3 tacking stitches. 4. Plunge the needle back down in the center of the pleat. Do not pull the thread tight.

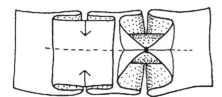

Fig. 4.21 Bring the edges of center-stitched box pleats together and tack them for a dimensional effect.

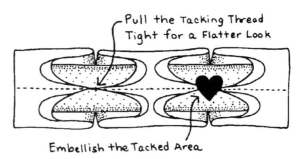

Fig. 4.23 Where the tacking thread is pulled tight, a flatter effect occurs. Embellish the tack.

Refer to Figure 4.22.

1. Bring the needle straight up from the bottom, in the middle of a center-stitched box pleat.

2. Pinch the edges of the pleat together at the center of the pleat.

3. Take two or three tiny tacking stitches to hold the edges together.

4. Return the needle down in the same place it came up. *Do not pull the thread tight.* Doing so will flatten the tacked pleat. Take a back stitch on the wrong side to lock the stitching before travelling to the next pleat. Let the tacking thread travel along the back of the pleated band or within the underfold area of the pleats.

In Step 4, the tacking thread was not pulled tight. Also try a few pleats with the thread pulled tight. It makes an interesting variation. (Figure 4.23.) Embellish the flattened tack area with a button or tiny rose.

One-side-tacked box pleats

This is an especially nice effect at the bottom edge of a box or basket. I used it at the bottom of the frosted cake shown in the color photographs. I like it best in ribbon about 7/8" wide.

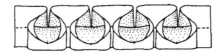

Fig. 4.24 One-side-tacked box pleats.

Make box pleats, center-stitched, but with the stitching line just a bit above center. Bring the middle of the top edge of each pleat down below the stitching line and tack it about halfway between the center and the bottom edge of the ribbon. (Figure 4.25.)

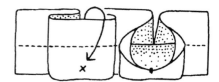

Fig. 4.25 Bring the top edge of the pleat to a point between the center stitching and bottom edge. Tack in place.

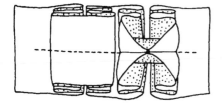

Double box pleats

These pleats can be made flat or tacked. (Figure 4.26.)

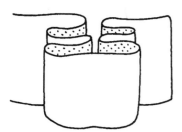

Fig. 4.26 *Double box pleats—flat and tacked.*

For tacked pleats, center stitch the band of pleats then tack them as shown in Figure 4.22 on page 42.

Double box pleats require ribbon five times the finished length.

Double box pleats by eye

Make two knife pleats on top of each other; then make two knife pleats on top of each other which face in the opposite direction. (Figure 4.27.)

Fig. 4.27 *To make a double box pleat by eye, make two knife pleats on top of each other facing in one direction, and two knife pleats on top of each other facing in the opposite direction.*

Double box pleats by the gauge method

Use nine 1/2" gauges. Refer to Figure 4.28. You may find it helpful to mark each gauge alphabetically from a to i.

1. Tack the righthand end of the ribbon to the foam-board pin board. Leaving at least 1" at the end, make two knife pleats on top of each other as in Steps 1 – 5 of Figure 4.19 on page 41.

2. Make two more knife pleats on top of the others using gauges "e","f","g", and "h", following Steps 1 – 5 of Figure 4.19 again.

Place gauge "i" on top of the ribbon directly over the other gauges.

3. Turn the frontfolds of the top two knife pleats to the left, letting gauge "e" drop away.

4. Remove gauges "a" through "d". Tack the right side of the pleat to the pin board with quilt pins at the top and bottom of the pleat. Leave the other gauges in place while making the next pleat.

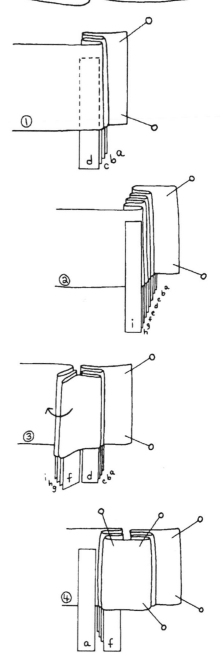

Fig. 4.28 *Double box pleats can be made quickly and evenly with gauges.*

Ribbon Origami Ornament

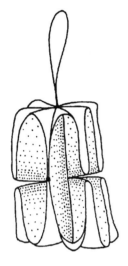

Fig. 4.29 *Create an ornament that looks like ribbon origami.*

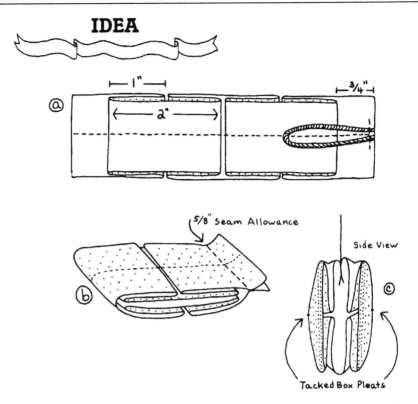

Fig. 4.30 *To make the ornament: a. Make two, 2" box pleats and center stitch. Baste a hanging loop in place. b. Fold the pleats, right sides together, and stitch across the ends. c. Turn pleats right side out and tack each pleat separately.*

Make an eye-catching ornament that looks like a complicated creation of ribbon origami. In reality, it is simply two tacked box pleats, folded to face in opposite directions. It is most stunning made in double-face, metallic novelty ribbon like the ones shown in the color photographs. The ornament on the right in the photograph is made of wire-edge ribbon.

Supplies
14" of 1-1/2"-wide ribbon (ornament)
6" of metallic embroidery thread or narrow ribbon (hanging loop)
White or neutral sewing thread
Seam sealant

Refer to Figure 4.30.

a. Cut both ends of the ribbon cleanly and treat both with seam sealant. Let dry. Leaving 3/4" of ribbon at each end, make two 2"-wide, full depth, box pleats next to each other. Baste the pleats well.

Center stitch from one end of the ribbon to the other.

Fold a 6" piece of metallic thread or narrow ribbon in half to form a loop. Baste this, as shown, at one end of the ribbon.

b. Fold the pleated ribbon in half, right sides together, so the two box pleats face in toward each other.

Stitch the ends together with a 5/8" seam allowance. Do not catch the pleats in the stitching line.

c. Turn the folded ribbon right side out, so the box pleats face in opposite directions. Tack each pleat.

Christmas Bell Pull 🔔🔔🔔

Supplies
2 yards, 1-1/2"-wide red
 grosgrain ribbon
2 yards, 7/8"-wide green
 grosgrain ribbon
Sewing thread to match
 each color ribbon
5/8" or 3/4" gold button
1-1/2"-diameter gold jingle
 bell
3/4" rustproof safety pin
Five 1"-wide cardboard
 gauges

1. Baste the green ribbon on top of the red ribbon, centering it.

2. Leaving a 6-1/2" end, make nine box pleats using 1" gauges. (If pleating by eye, make nine pleats, 2-1/8" wide.) (Figure 4.31.) Baste the pleats near the center.

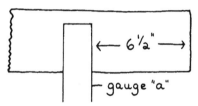

Fig. 4.31 Gauge placement for the first gauge.

3. Return to the 6-1/2" end (this will be the top of the bell pull), and make a 1" knife pleat with the frontfold facing the first box pleat. (If using gauges, place the first gauge,"a", next to the first box pleat.) (Figure 4.32.)

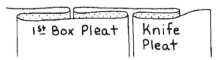

Fig. 4.32 Placement of the top knife pleat and the first box pleat.

4. Machine stitch through the center of the ribbon from end to end.

5. Turn the top end under 1/4" and fold it to the back to meet the back fold of the knife pleat. Hem.

6. Cut off the bottom end, leaving 3-1/2". Turn under the bottom end 1/4" and fold it to back to meet the last pleat. Hem.

7. Sew a button to the top of the bell pull as shown in Figure 4.33. Sew a bell to the bottom.

8. Attach a safety pin to back top of the bell pull to use as a hanger for the wall or a door.

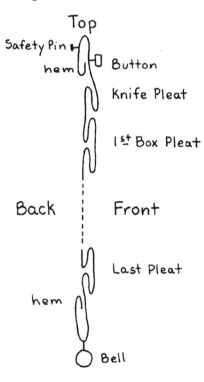

Fig. 4.33 Placement of details and finishes for the bell pull.

5. Ribbon Bows

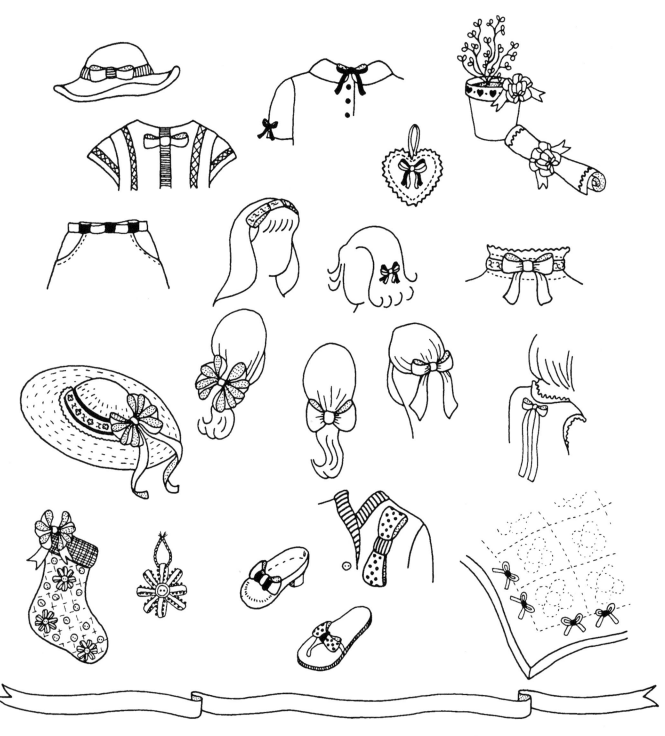

Bows add the perfect finish to hats, baskets, clothing and so much more. The bows in this chapter were selected for their versatility and because each is well-suited to woven-edge ribbon.

Some craft ribbons, especially those with a suppleness similar to woven-edge varieties, can be used as well.

Bow Basics

Bow Anatomy

Looking at the parts of a bow helps clarify terms used. Figure 5.1 shows two bows and their parts. It also illustrates the width and length terms used for the various bows.

Making Choices

Choosing the Variety of Ribbon to Use

Satin ribbon often comes to mind as a first choice for bows, but experiment with sheers, novelties, taffeta, Jacquards, grosgrain, wire-edge, picots, velvet, and even laces.

Choosing the Size and Kind of Bow

Look at the end use for the bow. To decorate a large gift basket filled with a variety of goodies, a large, overstated Rose Bow would be festive. A small Tied Bow at the top of a blouse might add the perfect touch of color to liven up a business outfit.

What About the Tails?

The tails are as important to a bow's appearance as its loops. If you are unsure how long you want them, plan them long—they can always be cut shorter.

Since woven ribbon frays when cut, tails should be cut on the bias to retard this tendency. Figure 5.3 shows two cuts often used, the **Diagonal** and the **Swallowtail**.

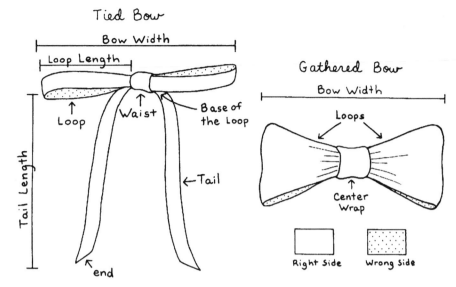

Fig. 5.1 Knowing the parts of the bow helps understand its construction.

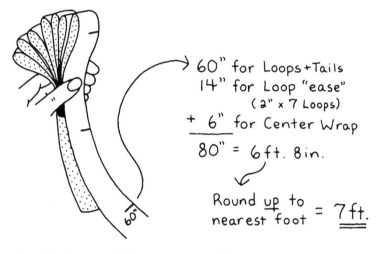

60" for Loops + Tails
14" for Loop "ease"
(2" x 7 Loops)
+ 6" for Center Wrap
80" = 6ft. 8in.

Round up to nearest foot = 7 ft.

Fig. 5.2 Use the Ribbon Estimating Tape to estimate the amount of yardage needed for a bow; shown is a Rose Bow estimate.

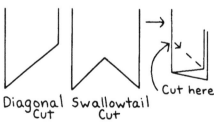

Diagonal Cut   Swallowtail Cut   Cut here

Fig. 5.3 Use a diagonal or swallow-tail cut on tail ends to retard fraying.

Estimating Yardage

Estimate yardage by making a prototype bow in your hand with the Ribbon Estimating Tape (page 10) or a tape measure. Figure 5.2 shows the process for a Rose Bow. Be sure to include the tails plus add "ease" for loop construction. Bows can be very deceptive—they usually take more ribbon than expected.

Hints for Easy Bow Making

1. Sometimes ribbon has a mind of its own—a loop won't face in the desired direction or one tail flies off to the side with an awkward look. It is *not* cheating to manipulate the loops and tails, tacking them in place with hidden stitches.

2. When using satin or other slippery ribbons, a few stitches on the back of the bow helps keep center wraps from moving, knots from undoing themselves over time, and satin faces facing out.

3. Use polyester or cotton-wrapped polyester thread for bow making. These have more strength than cotton. This is especially important for making bows like the Rose Bow, where the thread is subjected to a great deal of pulling.

4. Bow making is two-handed work. Before starting any bow, have a needle threaded with matching thread ready to pick up when needed. Stopping a bow midway to thread a needle is difficult.

5. Bows that go through the washer and dryer tend to lose their original liveliness. When possible, make them detachable (see page 9). Wash bows gently by hand, and only when necessary.

The Bows

The directions for each bow list the yardage and dimensions of the pictured bow. Most of them are shown in the color photographs as well.

The Traditional Bow

This is probably the most commonly made bow. It is a handy one because the loops and tails can be adjusted after it is finished. Use double-face ribbons such as satin, grosgrain, or soft taffeta.

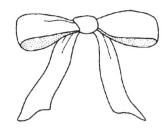

Fig. 5.4 *Traditional Bow.*

Ribbon: 48" of 1-1/2"-wide grosgrain

Bow Width: 6-1/2"

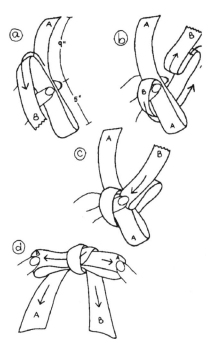

Fig. 5.5 *Making a Traditional Bow.*

Refer to Figure 5.5.

a. Make a 5" loop in End A, leaving a 9" tail. Pinch the ribbon at the point where the loop begins. Hold this with the left thumb and index finger.

b. Bring End B over the left thumb and under Loop A. Make a loop in End B.

c. Pull the loop in B through the center.

d. Adjust the size of the loops and tails and pull the knot tight.

Traditional Bow Variation

Two-color traditional bow

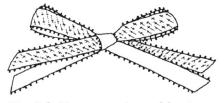

Fig. 5.6 *Use two colors of feather-edge satin together to make a pretty Traditional Bow variation.*

Ribbon:
16" of 3/8"-wide feather-edge satin, Color A

16" of 3/8"-wide feather-edge satin, Color B

Bow Width: 4"

Holding the two colors of ribbon together as if they were one, tie a Traditional Bow as shown in Figure 5.5. Leave a 3" tail at End A, and make a 2" loop.

The Tied Bow

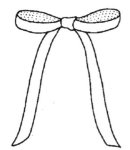

Fig. 5.7 *Tied Bow.*

The Tied Bow is usually reserved for ribbons 1" wide or less. Single- or double-face ribbon can be used, with satin being the usual choice. Silk ribbon and seam binding make dainty tiny bows. The Tied Bow is most easily tied around another person's two index fingers held apart. In a pinch, I have used the two spool posts on my sewing machine. For very tiny bows, use two quilt pins in the pin board. Because of the way this bow is tied, make all adjustments to center the knot, and pull it tight, before removing the bow from the fingers.

Ribbon: 20" of 5/8"-wide double-face satin

Bow Width: 4"

Refer to Figure 5.8.

a. Wrap the length of ribbon around an assistant's fingers from front to back, crossing the ends in the back so End B is behind End A.

b. Twist Ends A and B, so End A comes up and forward.

c. Make a knot, bringing End A around End B, as shown.

d. Pull the knot to the back as it is pulled tight. Make sure it is centered, making two identical size loops, before pulling the knot tight.

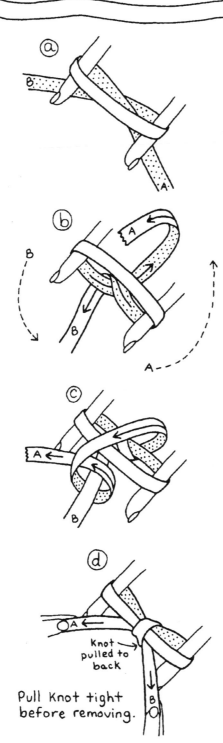

Fig. 5.8 *Making a Tied Bow.*

IDEA

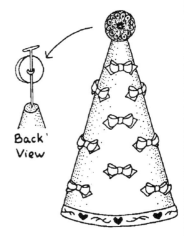

Bow Tree ☺☺☺

Fig. 5.9 *A styrofoam cone covered with felt becomes a Christmas tree table decoration when small tied bows of ribbon or seam binding are added.*

Make a bow tree for a quick table decoration. Glue green felt to cover a styrofoam cone. Glue a band of ribbon around the bottom of the cone. Make tiny 1" Tied Bows, using 6" of narrow ribbon or seam binding for each bow. Pin the bows to the tree with pleat pins. Top the tree with a gold button. Use a button with a shank and attach it to the tree top with a "T" pin. The tree as it is shown in the color photographs sits on a round felt mat with knotted ribbon fringe. (See page 84.) I chose Christmas colors, but pastel colors would be appropriate for an Easter centerpiece.

Tied Bow Variations

Two-color tied bow

Fig. 5.10 *Use two colors of ribbon together for an interesting Tied Bow variation.*

Holding two colors of ribbon together as if they were one, tie a bow following the diagrams in Figure 5.8 on page 49.

Multi-loop tied bow

Fig. 5.11 *Multi-Loop Tied Bow.*

Ribbon: 45" of 5/8"-wide single-face satin

Bow Width: 4" (three loops)

Follow the steps for the Tied Bow (see Figure 5.8), but add one or two additional wraps of the ribbon in Step a before finally crossing the ends.

The Loop Circle Bow

This bow is constructed in several parts. Four strips of ribbon make four loop sets which are tacked together to form a circle. The center is embellished with a button, rosebud, or a loop of ribbon. Make this bow from one color or several.

Thread a narrow ribbon or cord through one of the loops

Fig. 5.12 *Loop Circle Bow.*

of the bow and it instantly becomes a necklace or a Christmas ornament.

Ribbon: 38" of 3/8"-wide feather-edge satin

(Loop Strips: 9" each; Center Loop: 2")

Bow Width: 4"

Treat all loop strip ends with seam sealant before construction, as well as the ends of the center loop. With substantial ribbons such as feather-edge satin, keep a thimble handy to protect your fingers when sewing the several layers of ribbon together.

Refer to Figure 5.13.

a. Overlap the ends of each loop strip. Stitch the overlap with a tiny square of running stitches to hold them securely.

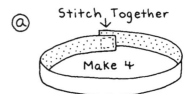

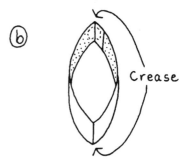

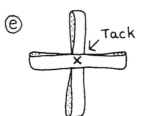

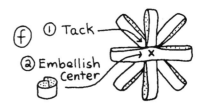

Fig. 5.13 *Making a Loop Circle Bow.*

b. Fold each circle in half crosswise to crease it at the center back (where the raw ends meet) and center front.

c. Bring the creases of each circle together.

d. Tack the creases together to form loops.

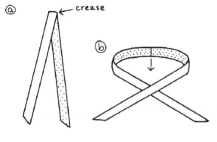

e. Tack two sets of loops together so they are perpendicular to each other. Use a cross-stitch tack to better hold the two pieces. Tack the other two sets together in the same way.

f. Tack the two pieces constructed in Step e together with a cross stitch. Make a tiny loop out of the remaining 2" piece of ribbon. Tack it to the center of the circle of loops either from the inside of the tiny loop or from the back.

Quickie Folded Bow

This quickly made little bow is ideal when several small,

Fig. 5.14 *Quickie Folded Bow.*

identical bows are needed. Double-face ribbon works best. Use ribbons 3/8"-wide or less for best results. Embellish the center of the bow with beads, a button, or a tiny flower.

Ribbon: 12" of 3/8"-wide feather-edge satin

Bow Width: 2-3/4"

Refer to Figure 5.15.

a. Fold the length of ribbon in half crosswise and crease it.

Fig. 5.15 *Making a Quickie Folded Bow.*

Cut the ends on the bias.

b. Cross the ends in front to form even-length tails. Bring the center back to meet the intersection of the two ends.

c. Tack all three layers of ribbon together and embellish.

The Pump Bow

This bow is named for one of its traditional uses—as a

Fig. 5.16 *Pump Bow.*

decoration on the toe of a woman's dress shoe, called a pump. Taffeta picot makes a simple bow with a bit of interest. Also try Jacquards, velvet, and grosgrain.

The Pump Bow is made in two parts. A loop strip is formed into a set of loops, and another piece of ribbon forms the center wrap. Treat all ends with seam sealant before construction.

Ribbon: 17" of 1-1/2"-wide brocade

(Loop Strip: 13"; Center Wrap: 4")

Bow Width: 6"

Refer to Figure 5.17.

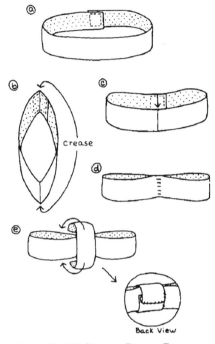

Fig. 5.17 *Making a Pump Bow.*

a. Overlap the ends of the loop strip to form a circle. Stitch the overlap with a little square of running stitches to hold it securely.

b. Fold the circle in half crosswise to crease it at the center back (where the raw ends overlap) and center front.

c. Bring the creases together.

d. Tack the creases together to form two loops.

e. Wrap the 4" center-wrap piece around the loop set with the raw ends to the back. Overlap the ends of the wrap. Turn under the top end and hem. If the ribbon is slippery, lock the center wrap in place with a couple of stitches into the back of one loop.

Pump Bow Variations:

Ribbon and lace pump

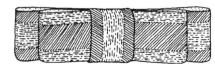

Fig. 5.18 Use ribbon and lace together on a Pump Bow.

Ribbon: 11-1/2" of 7/8"-wide grosgrain

(Loop Strip: 9"; Center Wrap: 2-1/2")

Lace: 9" of 1" flat lace or lace ribbon

Bow Width: 4"

Refer to Figure 5.17, constructing the loop set with ribbon and lace held together.

Double pump bow

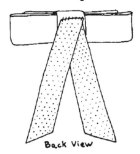

Fig. 5.19 Double Pump Bow in a double-face Jacquard.

Make two sets of loops, one longer than the other. Make them from the same ribbon or use two different colors, patterns, or varieties of ribbon or lace for added interest. The sample in the color photographs uses a double-face, gold-stripe Jacquard ribbon, reversing the faces.

Ribbon: 29" of 1-1/2"-wide ribbon

(Loop Strips: 10" & 14"; Center Wrap: 4-1/2")

Bow Width: 6-1/2"

Construct each loop set as shown in Figure 5.17 on page 51. Tack the two loop sets together in the center. Finish with a center wrap.

Pump bow with tails

Add tails to any Pump Bow for a pretty embellishment. The sample shown in the color photographs is a Double Pump Bow made entirely of velvet ribbon.

Ribbon: 28-1/4" of 1"-wide velvet

(Loop Strips: 7" & 8-1/2"; Center Wrap: 2-3/4"; Tails: 10")

Bow Width: 4"

After completing the center wrap of the Pump Bow, attach

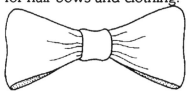

Fig. 5.20 Add tails to the back of any Pump Bow.

the tails. (Figure 5.20.) For double-face ribbon, simply fold the tail piece in half. For single-face ribbons, cut the piece in half and place both halves face out.

The Gathered Bow

The Gathered Bow is perfect for hair bows and clothing.

Fig. 5.21 Gathered Bow.

Like the Pump Bow, one length of ribbon makes the loops and another makes the center wrap.

Wider ribbons, 1-1/2"-wide and up, work best for the loops of the Gathered Bow. These widths, however, are often too wide for the center wrap. There are three alternatives: 1) search your scrap basket for a matching color piece in a narrower width ribbon; 2) purchase a length of narrower ribbon; 3) fold a length of the wide ribbon into a tube as shown in Figure 5.22a.

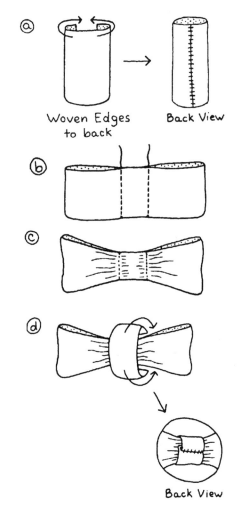

Fig. 5.22 Making a Gathered Bow.

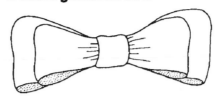

When gathering the loop strip, place a row of running stitches close to each edge of, but within the area covered by, the center wrap. Using these two rows of gathering gives the loops more character than having one row of gathering down the middle.

Ribbon: 12-1/2" of 1-1/2"-wide grosgrain

(Loop Strip: 10-1/2"; Center Wrap: 2")

Bow Width: 4-5/8"

Refer to Figure 5.22.

a. To make a center wrap from the wider ribbon: Fold the center wrap piece to bring the woven edges together. Overcast. Flatten the center wrap so the overcast seam is at the center back.

b. To make the loop set, overlap the ends of the loop strip to form a circle and stitch the overlap with a small square of running stitches. Fold the circle in half crosswise to crease it at center back and center front. Bring the creases together to form two loops. Tack the two layers together. (See Figure 5.17, Steps a – d on page 51.)

Lay the center wrap in place on the loop set. With a pencil, mark the loop set just inside each edge of the wrap.

Hand stitch two rows of gathering stitches from edge to edge on the loop piece, one row at each pencil mark.

c. Pull up the gathers.

d. Fold the center wrap around the bow with the raw ends overlapping at the back of the bow. Turn the top end under and hem.

Gathered Bow Variation

Double gathered bow

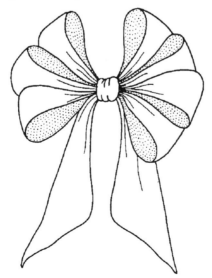

Fig. 5.23 Double Gathered Bow.

Ribbon:
10-1/2" of 1-1/2"-wide grosgrain, Color A

12" of 1-1/2"-wide grosgrain, Color B

3-1/2" of 1-1/2"-wide grosgrain for center wrap tube

Bow Width: 5-1/4"

Make two loop sets, one 4-1/4" wide and one 5-1/4" wide. Gather each separately as shown in Figure 5.22, then tack them together and add the center wrap.

The Rose Bow

This is one of the prettiest bows for woven-edge ribbon. Making these is like making teddy bears—each has its own personality.

Fig. 5.24 Rose Bow.

The secret to making the lovely loops in this bow is to gather up tiny pleats at the base of each loop, doing this *separately to each side of the loop* rather than gathering both sides together.

Another secret to a pleasing Rose Bow is to make an odd number of loops for variety. Use five, seven, or nine loops.

Ribbon: 2 yards of 2-1/4"-wide single-face satin

(Loop Length: 2-1/2"; Tail Length: 7")

Bow Width: 5-1/2"; seven Loops

Refer to Figure 5.25.

a. Leave 7" at End A for a tail and place your left thumb and index finger just above this 7" tail.

b. With the thumb and index fingers of both hands, gather up tiny, even pleats across the ribbon's face. As shown in the circle inset, take two tacking stitches in the edge of the ribbon. Do not cut the thread until the bow is finished.

c. Wrap the thread two times around the pleats and pull tight (but not so tight as to break the thread). As shown in the circle inset, take another two tacking stitches in the edge of the ribbon to hold the wraps tight. Turn the work over so the wrong side is facing you.

d. Form a 2-1/2" long loop by folding Length B forward on top of A. Make tiny, even pleats across the face at the base of the loop.

e. Wrap the thread twice around the pleats made in Step "d", as well as around the

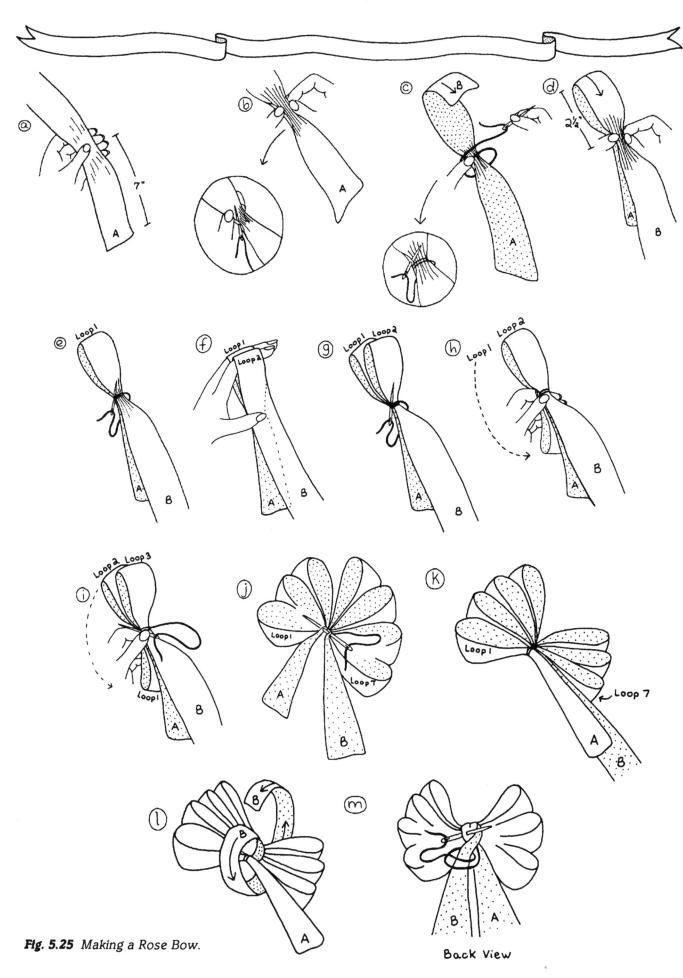

Fig. 5.25 Making a Rose Bow.

ones from Step "b". Have these wrappings fall directly on top of the ones previously made in Step "c". Take two tacking stitches in the edge of the ribbon. Loop 1 is now completed.

f. Bring sufficient ribbon up to form Loop 2.

Hint: To make each loop the same length, hold the previous loop taut with the left middle finger inserted in it. Use the left index finger to hold the ribbon for the present loop taut, gauging the appropriate place to make the pleats at the base of the loop.

g. Repeat Steps "d" and "e" to complete Loop 2.

h. Holding the base of Loops 1 and 2 in the left hand at the wrappings, fold Loop 1 down to meet Tail A, and hold it there while making the next loop.

As each loop is made, the previous one will be folded back to join Loop 1. This helps keep the thread wrappings in one place.

i. Complete Loop 3 by repeating Steps "d" and "e". Fold back Loop 2, as in Step "h", then make Loop 4. Continue this process until seven loops are completed.

Watch that the loops stay about the same size. They sometimes have a tendency to get smaller, especially at Loops 3 through 5.

j. With all the loops complete, hold the bow with its back toward you. Tack Loop 1 and Loop 7 together at the center.

k. Place End A on top of End B and Loop 7.

l. Wrap Length B over End A, around the center of the bow between Loops 4 and 5, then around to the front. As End B passes the front, twist it face out to form a pleasing center wrap. Bring End B all the way around to the back again.

m. Twist End B to form a tail with its face toward the front of the bow. Wrap Tail B with thread, then stitch into the back of the center wrap to lock it. Cut the thread.

Cut the tails on the bias. Adjust and fluff the loops and tails as needed for a pleasing appearance.

Rose Bows in Various Ribbons

Most any supple, drapeable ribbon makes a beautiful Rose Bow. The color photographs show Rose Bows in several ribbons: satin, grosgrain, wire-edge taffeta, and monofilament-edge sheer. See how each has its own personality! A mini Rose Bow makes a festive Christmas decoration.

Fig. 5.26 *Make a mini Rose Bow as a tree ornament.*

Magic Loop Bow

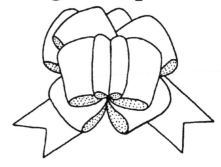

Fig. 5.27 *Magic Loop Bow.*

This machine-made bow is called Erica's Bow, designed by the Viking Sewing Machine Co. Since it creates loops like magic, I have called it the Magic Loop Bow.

Ribbon:
44" of 1-1/2"-wide single-face satin, cut ends on bias
44" of 1/4"- or 3/8"-wide single-face satin

Bow Width: 3-1/2"

Refer to Figure 5.28.

a. Fold both ribbons in half crosswise, with right sides facing out. Center the narrow ribbon inside the wider ribbon.

Stitch crosswise through all four layers of ribbon 1/8" in from the fold. Begin stitching 1/4" from one edge and stop 1/4" before the other edge. Lock the thread at both ends of the stitching line.

Mark the ribbon edges with little pencil marks at the intervals shown.

Make a machine stitched bar tack perpendicular to the edge at each mark. Be careful not to catch the narrow ribbon in the bar tacks.

If your machine does not have a bar tack setting, use a narrow zigzag with a zero stitch length and sew a few stitches in place. Alternatively,

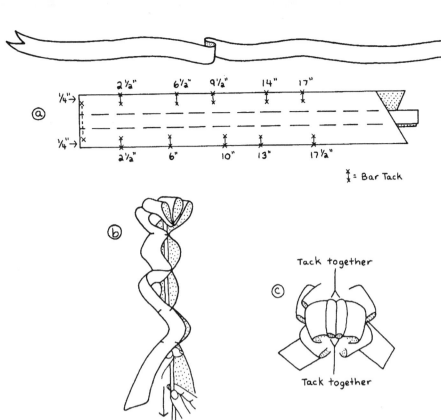

ⓐ

$\frac{1}{4}"\rightarrow$ 2½"   6½"   9½"   14"   17"

$\frac{1}{4}"\rightarrow$ 2½"   6"   10"   13"   17½"

$\updownarrow$ = Bar Tack

ⓑ

ⓒ

Tack together

Tack together

Fig. 5.28 *Making a Magic Loop Bow.*

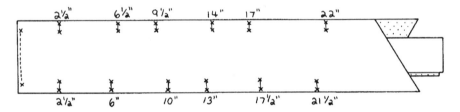

2½"   6½"   9½"   14"   17"   22"

2½"   6"   10"   13"   17½"   21½"

Fig. 5.29 *Measurements for a Magic Loop Bow in 2-1/4"-wide ribbon.*

sew a 3/8" line of straight machine stitching with a short stitch length, locking the thread at both ends.

b. Pull up the loops by pulling down on the ends of the narrow ribbons with the right thumb and index finger, while the left thumb and index finger, placed under the last bar tacks, push the loops up.

Lock the loops in place by hand stitching across the opening in the bottom of the bow, catching the narrow ribbon into the stitching. Use the narrow ribbon lengths as ties for the bow, or cut them off.

c. With some ribbons, the center two loops tend to fold with a crease rather than to form loops. If this occurs,

place tacking stitches at the base of the two center loops to hold them together.

Make this bow in wider ribbon as well. For a 4"-wide bow, use 50" of 2-1/4"-wide single-face satin and 50" of 3/8"-wide single-face satin. Mark the measurements shown in Figure 5.29.

Bow Band Border

Make a band of bows to decorate a basket, apron, pillowcase, or even a T-shirt. (Figure 5.31.) The band and

Fig. 5.30 *Bow Band Border.*

the bow loops are made from one length of ribbon. The center wrap and tails for each bow are made from one length. Add interest by using a different color for the center wrap and tails. A small basket in the color photographs is trimmed with a two-color Bow Band Border.

Fig. 5.31 *Add a Bow Band Border to baskets, shirts, skirts, and even pillowcases.*

Ribbon:
31" of 3/8"-wide single-face
satin for band
32" of 3/8"-wide single-face
satin for tails/center wrap

Bow Width: 2"; Space Between Bows: 1"

Tail Length: 2-1/8"; Band
Length: 15"

These measurements make a practice band of four bows. Refer to Figure 5.32.

a. Mark the ribbon at the intervals shown with light pencil marks at the edges.

b. With the right side of the ribbon facing out, bring the beginning and end mark of each 4" interval together. Machine stitch crosswise at the marks, locking the stitches at each edge and trimming threads. Hold the ribbon taut while stitching to prevent it from being pulled into the hole in the needle plate.
Stand the loops upright and crease each at the top.

c. Finger press the crease down to meet the stitched seam below. Machine stitch across the crease, again holding the ribbon taut while stitching. Lock the stitches at both edges and trim threads.

d. Cut the tail/center wrap ribbon into 8" lengths. With the ribbon face out, wrap a raw end to the back of the band, centering it over the machine stitching at the center of the bow loops. Hand stitch it in place with a little square of running stitches that do not show through to the front of the bow. Wrap the ribbon

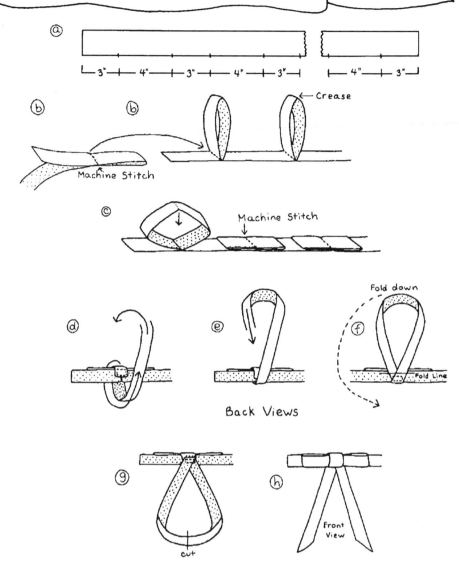

Fig. 5.32 Making a Bow Band Border.

length to the back of the band as shown.

e. Make a loop in the tail/center wrap piece as shown, with the face toward the back of the bow.

f. Tuck the raw end under the first part of the loop in the tail/center wrap piece. Hand stitch in place with a small square of running stitches that do not shown through to the front. Fold the tail loop down on the fold line shown on the diagram. The face of the ribbon should now be facing toward

the front of the bow.

g. Hand stitch the tails in place on the back of the bow, just below the fold, with a small square of running stitches that do not show through to the front. Cut the tail loop in the middle.

h. Even up the tail ends and cut them on the bias.

To calculate yardage for a bow band border, see Figure 5.33 on the following page.

Estimating Yardage for a Bow Band Border

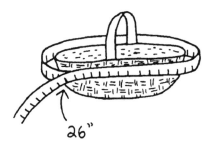

1. Using a tape measure, determine how long the band must be. This is the yardage needed for the band.

Band Yardage = 26"

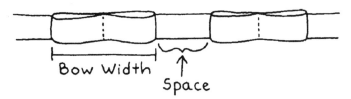

26"

2. Choose the bow width and spaces between bows.

Bow Width

Space

Example: Bow Width = 2"
            Space = 1"

3. Using quilt pins, mark the bow widths and spaces be- tween bows on the Ribbon Estimating Tape. Start with a space. How many bows fit on the band?

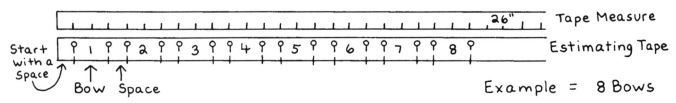

26"   Tape Measure

Start with a Space

Estimating Tape

Bow   Space

Example = 8 Bows

4. Calculate total bow yardage. Each bow requires 2 times the bow width. Each 2" bow = 4" yardage.

4" x 8 bows = 32"

Bow yardage = 32"

5. Calculate total yardage for center wrap/tail pieces by actually folding one with a tape measure around ribbon.

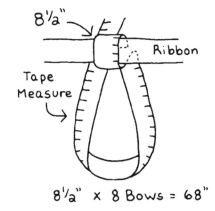

8½"

Ribbon

Tape Measure

8½" x 8 Bows = 68"

6. Figure total yardage needed and round up to the next foot.

a. One color border -

Band = 26"
+ Bows = 32"
+ Wrap/Tails = 68"
_____
126" (11 feet)

b. Two color border -

Color 1:
Band = 26"
+ Bows = 32"
_____
58" (5 feet)

Color 2:
Wrap/Tails = 68" (6 feet)

Fig. 5.33 Yardage calculations for a Bow Band Border.

Bow Angel ᗢᗢᗢᗢ

This little angel has a metallic ribbon bow for her wings. She is embellished with dabs and snippets from my favorite source—the scrap basket. Adorn her with odds and ends of ribbon and other findings to personalize her for yourself or a friend.

Depending on the ribbon you choose, consider the Pump Bows, a Traditional Bow, or a Gathered Bow for the wings. Since the ribbon I chose is not supple enough to gather well, I made a Double Pump Bow.

Supplies

9" x 12" white, medium-weight cloth

29" of 1-1/2"-wide metallic/iridescent novelty ribbon (or sufficient for the bow you have chosen)

Small scrap of tan felt

Polyester fiber stuffing

Red crayon

Pearl cotton or floss for eyes and mouth

Embellishments of your choice

White glue

a. Trace the patterns shown in Figure 5.35. Cut two body pieces and four arm pieces from the white fabric, and one face and two hands from felt.

b. Place two arm pieces together with right sides together. With a 1/4" seam allowance, stitch around the arm pieces leaving an opening between the circles. (Figure 5.36.) Clip corners and turn right side out. Repeat for other arm piece.

Fig. 5.34 Use a metallic ribbon bow for the Bow Angel's wings. Decorate her dress with tidbits from your scrap basket.

c. Place the arms on the right side of one of the body pieces so the open end is at the edge of the body. Baste the arms in place. (Figure 5.35.)

d. With right sides together and a 1/4" seam allowance, stitch around the body pieces, leaving an opening between the circles. For easier stitching, stitch both sides separately, starting at the "X" shown in Figure 5.36. Clip curves and corners and turn the body right-side-out.

e. Stuff with polyester stuffing, but do not overfill. Stitch the opening closed.

f. On the face, embroider each eye with two stitches and a French knot, and the mouth with two stitches, as shown on the pattern in Figure 5.35.

To make the cheeks, place the felt circle face up on a hard surface. Place the flat end of a red crayon on the felt where the cheek should be. While holding the face taut, press

down and turn the crayon one rotation. (Figure 5.37.) Repeat for the other cheek. (Practice this first on a scrap of felt to get the right pressure.)

g. Using white glue, attach the face, placing it as shown on the pattern. (Figure 5.35.)

h. Add embellishments to the skirt and sleeves. Once embellished, tack the sleeves to the middle front of the body and glue or stitch the hands inside the sleeve. (See Figure 5.35, dotted line.)

i. Add hair. Possibilities include 1-1/16"-wide silk ribbon ruffles, tiny curled ribbon, yarn, craft hair, or even baby rick rack.

j. Add a halo. I glued together the ends of a 5-1/2" length of gold loop trim, which was threaded with 28-gauge brass wire to help hold the circular shape.

k. Make the bow for wings. My Double Pump Bow (see page 52) has an overall bow width of 5-1/4". The smaller set of loops has a width of 4-1/2". (I used loop strips of 10" and 13", with an additional 5-1/2" for the center wrap.)

For the bow to look right from the front of the angel, it was made with the smaller set of loops nearest the back of the center wrap. In other words, just the opposite of the usual double pump bow. Placement of the wings is shown on the pattern. (Figure 5.35.)

l. Add a loop to the back if the angel is to be a tree ornament.

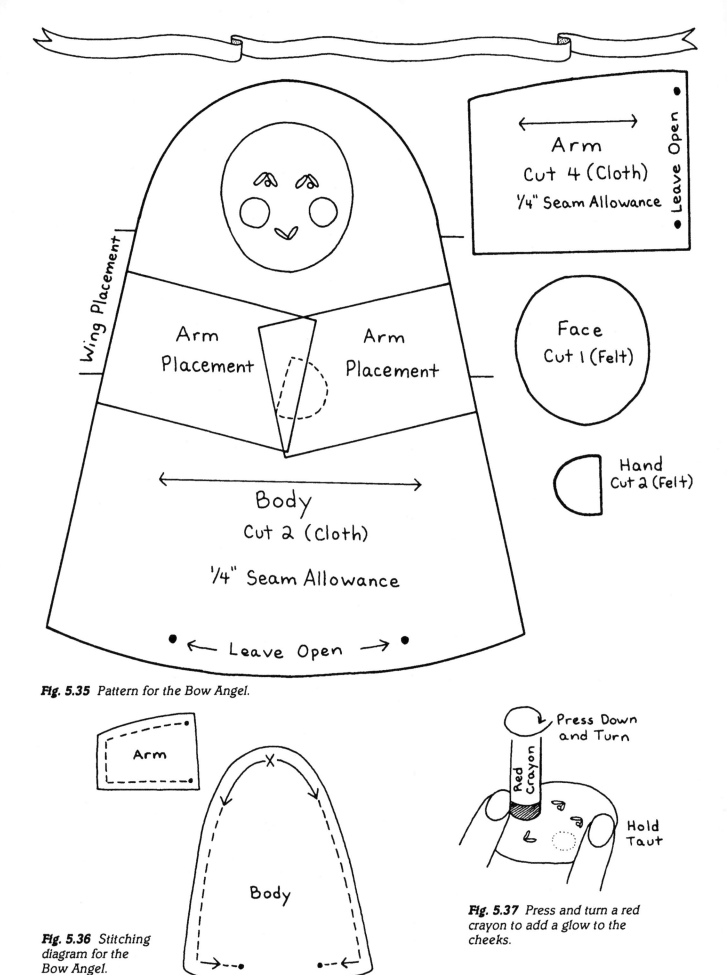

Fig. 5.35 Pattern for the Bow Angel.

Arm
Cut 4 (Cloth)
¼" Seam Allowance
• Leave Open

Wing Placement

Arm Placement

Arm Placement

Face
Cut 1 (Felt)

Hand
Cut 2 (Felt)

Body
Cut 2 (Cloth)

¼" Seam Allowance

• ← Leave Open →

Arm

X

Body

Fig. 5.36 Stitching diagram for the Bow Angel.

Press Down and Turn

Red Crayon

Hold Taut

Fig. 5.37 Press and turn a red crayon to add a glow to the cheeks.

6. Ribbon Flowers

Single Bloom

Clusters

Scattered

Ribbon flowers are delightful creations that range from realistic to imaginary. Use them on hair bands, sweaters, baskets, pockets, and collars. Scatter them, cluster them, or showcase one bloom.

The flowers are arranged according to their construction method. One of the pleasures of making ribbon flowers is that no two come out looking exactly alike. Suggested yardages are given for each flower as a starting point. Adjust

them as needed for your working style and preference.

Suggested leaf options are given for each flower. Refer to the section on leaves later in the chapter (starting on page 75).

Flower Making Basics

Choosing Ribbon

Any soft ribbon is fair game. Use both single- and double-face ribbons. Experiment with different varieties, colors, and patterns of ribbon. Try gingham sweet peas and polkadot poppies. Why not daisies in plaid or velvet, and roses of sheers or metallic novelties? Be sure to include picot- and wire-edge ribbons as well. Most of the flowers require little yardage, so check your scrap basket for inspiration.

Use narrow ribbons or seam binding for miniature flowers, and wider ribbons for larger ones. (Figure 6.1.)

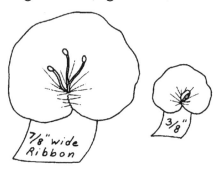

Fig. 6.1 *Use narrow ribbon for small flowers and wider ribbon for larger ones.*

Especially for rolled and gathered flowers, choose the most supple ribbons. Just because a ribbon is woven-edge does not mean it will make the prettiest flower. Even satins can range from crisp to soft. Opt for the softer ones.

Match materials and application methods to the care the finished project will require, or make the flowers detachable (see page 9).

Making Choices for Finishing Touches

Depending on the flower being made, the addition of leaves, centers, and/or stems will present a more complete effect. (Figure 6.2.) Separate instructions on finishing flower bases, stems, leaves, and centers follow the presentation of the flowers. Be familiar with the choices available before constructing the flowers.

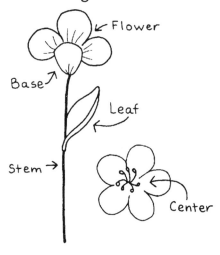

Fig. 6.2 *Knowing the parts of a ribbon flower helps plan its construction.*

Stems and stamens are added while constructing the flower. The base is then finished and leaves added.

Not all flowers need realistic-looking finishing touches. Be open to experiment. For example, when I first made a knotted daisy (Figure 6.19 on page 70), I tried various leaves but none gave the effect I wanted. The flower reminded me of the elaborate centers often seen on award ribbons. With that in mind, I played with folds and loops in a long piece of wire-edge taffeta until I came upon the motif in Figure 6.20e on page 70.

Hints for Easy Flower Making

1. Have a needle with knotted thread ready before starting a flower or leaf. Both hands will be too busy in the construction process to stop and thread a needle.

2. Use more thread than seems necessary, especially for flowers like rolled roses that will be tacked with each layer and finished by wrapping the thread. It is amazing how much thread even a small rose can consume.

3. Use polyester or cotton-wrapped polyester thread of matching or neutral color. 100% cotton thread is not strong enough to tack layers, tightly gather, or wrap bases.

4. Keep quilt pins and a foam-board pin board available. If the phone rings when you are halfway through a flower, tack it to the board so your work is not lost.

5. Keep white glue and wash-able glue handy to seal raw ends as soon as a flower or leaf is finished. Trim stray threads and even up the ends before gluing.

Rolled Rose

Fig. 6.3 *Rolled Rose.*

Satin is the first choice for rolled roses. Experiment also with taffeta, silk, seam binding, and even metallics and grosgrain. Make big roses and mini ones. Use Leaf #2 or #3 (see page 75-76).

A rolled rose involves folding the ribbon so that both sides show at different stages. It is tempting to believe a double-face satin is necessary. The interest created by having the shiny contrasted with the dull of a single-face ribbon is, however, attractive. Try both kinds of ribbon.

The yardage needed depends on how tight or loose the rolls and how many rolls are desired. Make rosebuds with just a few tight rolls, or full-blown roses with many loose rolls.

If a cluster of roses is desired, make each flower then wrap or stitch all of their bases together.

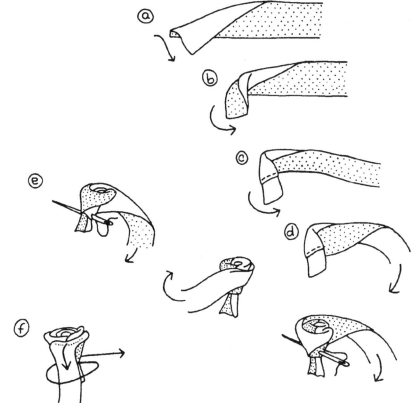

Fig. 6.4 *Making a rolled rose.*

Mini Rose: 2" – 3" of 3/8"-wide ribbon
Small Rose: 4" of 5/8"-wide ribbon
Medium Rose: 6" of 7/8"-wide ribbon
Large Rose: 18" of 1-1/2"-wide ribbon

Refer to Figure 6.4.

a. At one end of the ribbon length, with the wrong side of the ribbon facing up, fold the top edge toward you to create a diagonal fold, as shown.

b. Roll the folded end in on itself once.

c. Roll the ribbon in the same manner until the end of the fold is near. Tack the layers together. This serves as the center of the rose.

d. Now fold the top edge of the ribbon *away* from you so the wrong side turns to the back of the fold and the right side of the ribbon faces you below the fold.

e. Roll the folded length around the center one revolution. Tack through all layers. Continue folding the ribbon length to the back and rolling the ribbon. Tack after each revolution.

f. To end, fold the raw end down toward the bottom of the rose. Tack it in place. Wrap the thread around the base of the rose several times.

Flat Ribbon Rose

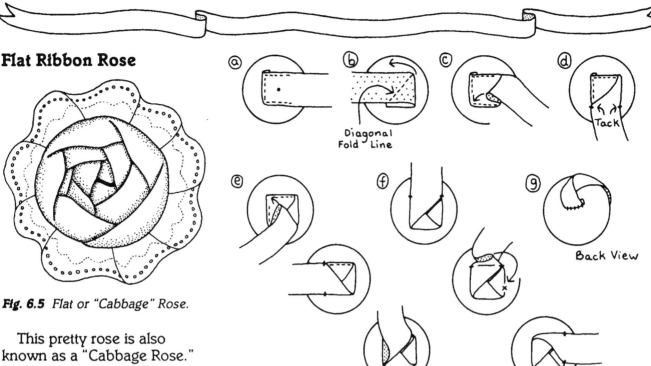

Fig. 6.5 Flat or "Cabbage" Rose.

This pretty rose is also known as a "Cabbage Rose." Single-face satin ribbon is ideal. Rather than use a leaf, I mount it on an eyelet rosette. I form the rosette from ready-made eyelet ruffle trim which I gather again by hand to make the gathering a little tighter.

The Flat Ribbon Rose is constructed by folding and tacking ribbon to a circular base and moving out toward the edge of the circle with each revolution. Use stiff, non-woven interfacing as a base. Felt can be used, but it is sometimes difficult to tack the outer rolls to the felt since its edges are fragile. The amount of ribbon needed depends on how tightly the folds are made and how quickly each turn moves out toward the edge of the circle.

> 1" diameter rose: 12" of
> 5/8"-wide ribbon
> 1-1/2" diameter rose: 14" of
> 5/8"-wide ribbon
> 2" diameter rose: 26" of
> 7/8"-wide ribbon

The instructions use a 2"

Fig. 6.6 Making a Flat Ribbon rose.

rose as an example. Refer to Figure 6.6.

a. Cut a 2" diameter circle of stiff interfacing.

Turn under one end of the ribbon and stitch the end and edges in the center of the base. This forms the center of the rose.

b. Fold the ribbon to the left, across the center.

c. Make a diagonal fold in the ribbon, as shown by the dotted line in Step "b", and bring the ribbon length back to the right.

d. Tack both edges to the base to hold the fold in place, as shown. Take the needle down to the back so it is ready to travel to the next stitch.

e. Fold the ribbon up over the center, then to the left on a diagonal, as before. Tack it to the base. Make the next fold taking the ribbon to the right over the center, then up on a diagonal fold.

f. Tack the fold and continue on, starting another revolution of folds. Continue until the base is covered.

Hint: Soften the angles of the ribbon while moving toward the circle's edge. Adjust the placement of the tacking stitches so each fold lays nicely but the stitches are covered by the next folds.

On the final folds, let the edge of the ribbon cover the outer edge of the base. Tack the ribbon edge to the edge of the base where appropriate to keep the rounded outline.

g. Fold the ribbon end to the back of the base. Turn it under and stitch in place.

Attach the rose to the rosette with blind stitches that catch the outer edge of the flower.

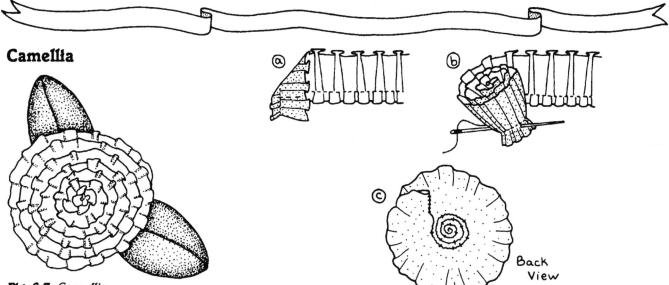

Camellia

Fig. 6.7 *Camellia.*

Fig. 6.8 *Making a camellia with prepleated single-face satin ribbon.*

Roll long lengths of gathered or pleated ribbon to create full blown flowers with an informal air. They remind me of camellias or sometimes, roses. Use a realistic leaf like #1, or a stylized one like #4 (see page 75).

Gather or pleat single-face satin ribbon, or purchase ready-made pleated or gathered lengths. Also try lengths of ready-made eyelet ruffle trim or gather a folded-over strip of 6"-wide tulle ribbon or lightweight fabric. Gathered wire- or picot-edge ribbons work well too. The color photographs display an off-white camellia of ready-made,

box-pleated ribbon, a red camellia of wire-edge taffeta, and a pink tulle rose. The tulle rose is finished with knotted ribbon streamers instead of leaves. (See Figure 7.10 on page 84.)

Ready-made ribbon camellia: 1 yard of 7/8"-wide ready-made box-pleated ribbon
Wire-Edge Camellia: 1 – 1-1/2 yards of 1-1/2"-wide wire-edge taffeta
Tulle Rose: 1 – 1-1/2 yards of 6"-wide tulle ribbon, folded in half lengthwise and loosely hand-gathered

Refer to Figure 6.8.

a. With right sides facing up, fold down one raw end on the bias and stitch it in place.

b. Roll the ribbon around this center with the right side of the ribbon facing toward the center.

With each revolution, tack the bottom edge of the ribbon to the previous revolutions. Every few revolutions, take a stitch through all of the layers.

c. Turn under the final end and stitch it to the previous layer of ribbon.

Gathered Flowers

Gathered flowers are usually gathered tightly and by hand.

Use a generous-sized knot to begin the gathering line and take a few small stitches so

the knot will not pull out in the gathering process.

Poppy

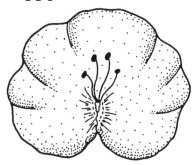

Fig. 6.9 *Poppy.*

Make poppies in grosgrain, satin, or taffeta. Make realistic ones in orange grosgrain or imaginary ones in prints and patterns. Add stamens to complete the flower. I don't usually add a leaf to poppies. Leaf #6 (see page 77), however, complements imaginary poppies such as the pink stripe moiré taffeta one shown in the color photographs.

Medium Poppy: 5-1/2" of
   5/8"-wide ribbon
Large Poppy: 6-1/2" of
   7/8"-wide ribbon
Extra Large Poppy: 8" of
   1-1/2"-wide ribbon

Refer to Figure 6.10.

a. With matching polyester thread, hand stitch a row of gathering stitches, as shown.

b. Pull up the gathers tightly. For a flatter flower, keep the gathers a little looser. Tighten them fully for a cupped flower. Stitch into the edge of the ribbon several times to lock the gathers.

c. If stamens are desired, tack them to the middle of the gathers, as shown. Bring points "x" and "y" around together. The raw ends will tend to fold toward the back of the flower, creating the "dimple" in the bottom of the poppy.

d. Tack the edges together. Wrap the ribbon where it was tacked. Cut the excess off the raw ends and seal with glue.

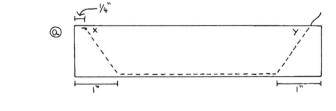

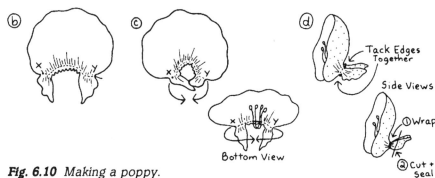

Fig. 6.10 *Making a poppy.*

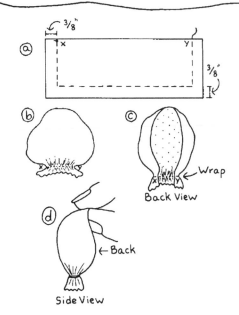

Sweet Pea

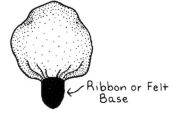

Fig. 6.11 *Sweet Pea.*

Start with single-face satin ribbon, but experiment with different ribbon varieties, prints and patterns for sweet peas. Plan to use a stem, as sweet peas look incomplete without one. Make freestanding ones with wire stems and attach ones with ribbon stems to a foundation. See Figure 6.24 on page 72.)

Fig. 6.12 *Making a sweet pea.*

Sweet Pea: 4" of 1-1/2"-wide ribbon

Refer to Figure 6.12.

a. Hand stitch a row of gathering stitches, as shown.

b. Pull up the gathers tightly to create a rounded shape with a top edge that cups to the back. Add in a stem at this point. (See Figures 6.25, 6.28 on pages 72 and 73.)

c. Bring the gathers in toward the center for wrapping. Edges "x" and "y" can be brought together or left a bit apart. Each choice gives a different effect.

d. Adjust the top edge of the ribbon so it cups nicely to the back.

Finish the base of the flower with ribbon or felt. (See page 74.)

Primrose

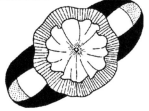

Fig. 6.13 *Primrose.*

Add these quick, floppy flowers with a sunny yellow center to hat bands and barrettes. Use Leaf #5 (see page 77). Stamens are not essential, but can certainly be added.

Primrose: 9" of 7/8"-wide yellow grosgrain, *and* 9" of 1-1/2"-wide pink or purple grosgrain

Refer to Figure 6.14.

a. Align the yellow ribbon on top and along one edge of the wider ribbon.

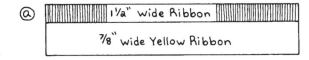

Fig. 6.14 *Making a primrose.*

b. Fold the ribbons in half crosswise, right sides together. Machine stitch the ends together, through all layers, using a 1/4" seam allowance. Cut the seam allowance to 1/8" and overcast with a zigzag stitch in matching pink or purple thread.

c. Hand stitch a row of gathering stitches along the bottom edge of each length of ribbon

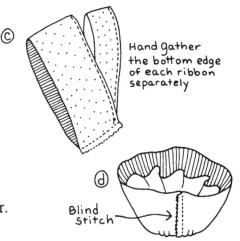

separately. Pull up the gathers on each length, pulling the gathers tighter on the yellow ribbon than on the other one.

d. Fold the overcast ends to the right or left and blind stitch to the back side of the pink or purple ribbon.

Spring Blossoms

Fig. 6.15 *Spring Blossom.*

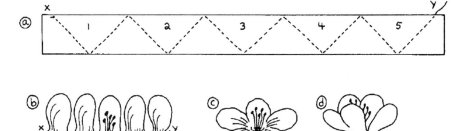

Fig. 6.16 *Making a spring blossom.*

These are usually just called "Five Petal" flowers, but they remind me of the tree blossoms of spring.

Use a soft, *very thin* ribbon. Ideal are soft polyester and silk taffetas, or single-face satin. Make mini ones in narrow silk or seam binding. In the color photographs, a tiny spring blossom is displayed on the silk ribbon sampler.

Stamens are usually added to the center of these flowers. Make free-standing blossoms with wire stems or attach them with or without ribbon stems to a foundation. Leaf #1 (see page 75) complements blossoms without stems.

Shell ruffles form the basis of the flower.

Small blossom: 6" of 1/2"-wide ribbon or seam binding

Medium blossom: 11" of 7/8"-wide ribbon

Large Blossom: 15" of 1-1/2"-wide ribbon

Refer to Figure 6.16.

a. Press bias fold creases to create five shells at one edge and four at the other edge. Gather the length as for Shell Ruffles. (See Figure 3.20 on page 31.) Machine gather wide ribbons, but hand gather silk ribbon, seam binding, and ribbons less than 7/8" wide.

b. Pull up the gathers tightly and knot the end of the thread. Hold the length with the five shells at the top. These will become the blossom's petals. The others will become the base.

Prepare stamens and tack them to the middle petal just below the gathering line. Add a stem at this point, if desired. (See Figures 6.25 and 6.28 on pages 72 and 73.)

c. Bring the two ends of the ribbon, "x" and "y", around to meet and tack them together.

d. Wrap thread tightly around the gathering line.

For a flatter flower to be attached to a foundation without stems, cut off the ribbon just below the wrapping and seal with glue. Otherwise, wrap the base of the flower in ribbon or green felt. (See page 74.)

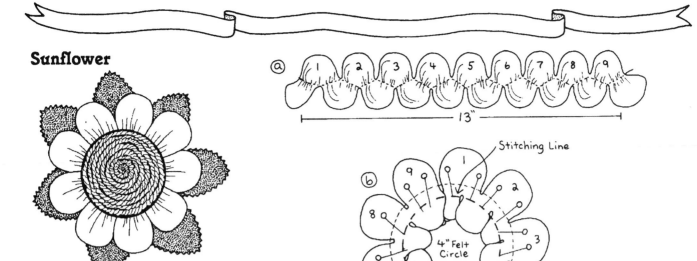

Sunflower

Fig. 6.17 *Sunflower.*

Bright yellow shell ruffles form the sunflower's petals, and a tight ruffle of brown seam binding decorates the center. The flower has about a 5" total diameter. Use one to decorate the top of a small round basket lid. (See page 61.)

> Sunflower: 30" of 1-1/2"-wide yellow grosgrain (petals)
> 4" circle of yellow felt (base)
> 3-1/4" circle of orange felt (center)
> 2 yards brown seam binding (center)
> Scrap of green felt (leaves)
> Polyester fiber stuffing

Refer to Figure 6.18.

a. Leaving 1" at the beginning and end of the yellow ribbon, make a Shell Ruffle (see page 31) with nine shells above and eight or nine below the gathering line. The finished band of shells should measure about 13" long.

Fig. 6.18 *Make a sunflower on a pin board.*

b. Tack the 4" yellow felt circle to the foam-board pin board with quilt pins.

Place one end of the Shell Trim on the felt circle. Fold the raw end to the center of the circle. Pin the Shell Trim around the circle so the gathering line is about 1/4" in from the edge of the felt all the way around. Pull up the gathers if needed to make the outer ring of shells fit around the circle.

Fold the last end toward the center of the circle. Hand stitch the ruffle to the felt inside of the gathering line, using yellow thread.

Fill the very center of the flower with a bit of polyester fiber stuffing to the height of the inner circle of shells.

c. Center the orange felt circle over the top. Baste it in place. This may require bending the petals and yellow felt circle in just a bit while basting so the orange circle covers the gath-

ering line on the yellow ribbon. This creates more lively petals.

Stitch the orange circle in place with blind stitches about 1/8" in from the edge of the orange circle.

d. Center-gather 2-1/2 yards of brown seam binding and pull up to make a 38" ruffle. Tack this to the felt in a spiral, starting in the center and working out to the edge of the circle.

Cut off any yellow felt from the back that shows to the front of the flower.

e. Using pinking shears and the pattern labelled "Sunflower" in Figure 6.32 on page 77, cut seven green felt leaves. Glue or stitch the leaves to the back of the flower so the edges show beyond the yellow petals.

Knotted Daisy

Fig. 6.19 *Knotted Daisy.*

Fig. 6.20 *Making a knotted daisy.*

Satin ribbon is perfect for this flower. If single-face is used, be sure the faces are turned to show on the front of the flower. The loops that make up this flower are stitched to a base of stiff, non-woven interfacing or felt. A disk-like center finishes it. (See Figure 6.30 on page 74.) Use a large leaf such as Leaf #4 (see page 76), or make the folded motif shown in Figure 6.20e.

Knotted Daisy: 5 yards of 1/4"- or 3/8"-wide single- or double-face satin

Refer to Figure 6.20.

a. Cut the ribbon into 36 lengths, each 5" long.

Knot each piece in the center with an overhand knot.

b. Fold each piece in half to form a loop with a satin face facing up and the ends over-lapped. Pin the overlap with a pleat pin.

c. Line up 18 loops along the edge of a length of adding-machine paper or tear-away stabilizer. Re-pin each loop to the paper, keeping the ends overlapped and overlapping each loop just slightly on top of the one before it. Set up the other 18 loops in the same manner on a separate strip of paper or stabilizer.

Using a short stitch length, machine stitch the ends of the loops on each strip, 1/4" in from the edge of the paper or stabilizer. Back stitch across the first and last loop on each strip to lock the stitches. Remove the paper or stabilizer so only the stitching holds each row of loops together.

Hint: Crease the paper along the stitching line and it pulls away easily.

d. Form each row into a circle of loops by bringing the first and last loop of each row together. Overlap them and stitch. Stitch one circle of loops to a small circle of felt or stiff non-woven interfacing. Place the other loop circle on top of the first one and stitch it in place.

Cover the center with a large button or an embellished felt circle.

e. To make the folded leaf motif: Use 1 yard of 7/8"-wide dark green, wire-edge taffeta and fold the motif as shown. Tack the layers of the motif together in the center. Stitch or glue it to the back of the flower.

Some ribbons such as velvet and grosgrain do not knot well. They can still be used to make the daisy—just omit the knot. The daisy can also be made with more or less loops, as desired.

Rolled Loop Daisy

Fig. 6.21 Rolled Daisy.

Make this informal daisy in a substantial ribbon such as velvet or grosgrain. Use as many loops as desired. Stamens can be added but are not essential. Finish with a ribbon base (see page 74) and add large leaves such as Leaf #4 or #5 (see page 76).

Rolled Daisy: For a 12-loop daisy: 60" of 1/4"- or 3/8"-wide ribbon

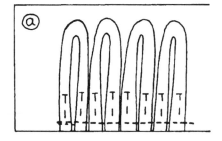

Fig. 6.22 Making a rolled daisy.

Refer to Figure 6.22.

a. Cut the ribbon into 12 lengths, each 5".

b. Fold each into a loop, but do not overlap the ends.
   Line up all of the loops along the edge of a length of adding-machine paper or tear-away stabilizer. Pin them next to each other without overlapping ends or overlapping the loops.
   Using a short stitch length, machine stitch the ends of the

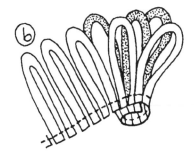

loops 1/4" in from the edge of the paper. Back stitch across the first and last loop to lock the stitches. Remove the paper or stabilizer so only the stitching holds the loops together.

Hint: Crease the paper along the stitching line and it pulls away easily.

c. Roll the loops so they fall away from the center of the flower with their faces up. With each revolution, stitch through all layers in the flower base.

Knotted Dahlia

Fig. 6.23 Knotted Dahlia.

When many knotted loops of satin ribbon are rolled around each other, a dahlia results. This flower requires no center. Use large leaves such as Leaf #4 (see page 76).

Knotted Dahlia: 8-1/2 yards of 1/4"- or 3/8"-wide satin ribbon

a. Cut the ribbon into 60 lengths, 5" each.
   Knot each as shown in Figure 6.20a on page 70.

b. In the same manner as the Rolled Loop Daisy, make loops, set them up, and stitch and roll them (See Figure 6.22).

Completing Flowers With Stems, Centers, Bases, and Leaves

Stems

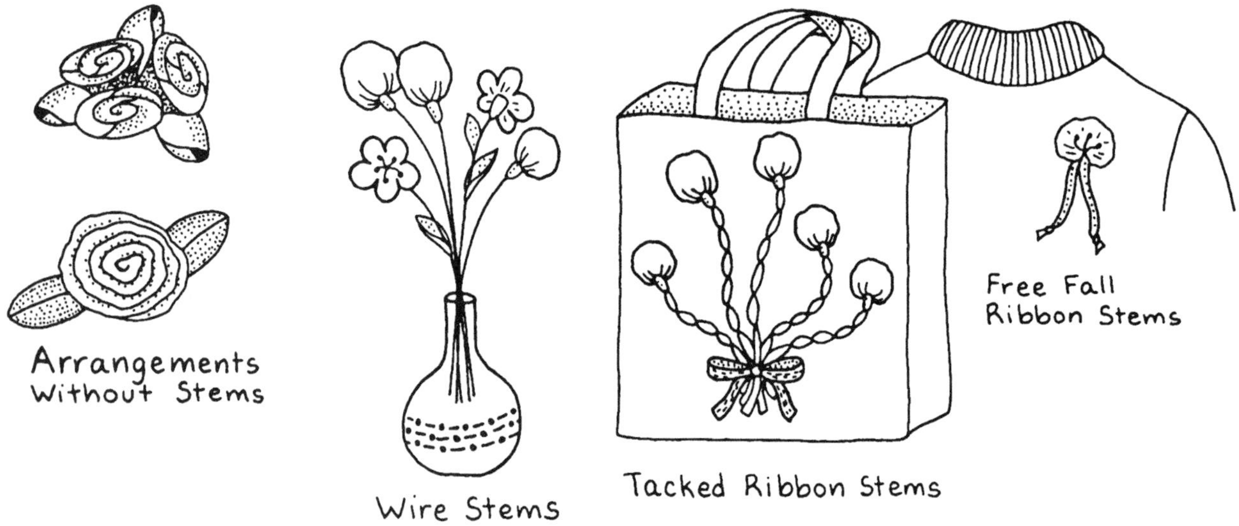

Fig. 6.24 *There are various stem possibilities and some flowers need none at all.*

Often stems are not needed because flowers are attached in clusters or individually with just a few leaves. Ribbon flowers can, however, have several kinds of stems. (Figure 6.24.)

Attach stems to the base of the flower while it is under construction and before finishing the flower base.

Wire Stems

For freestanding sweet peas or spring blossoms, use green, wrapped floral wire stems, available in several thicknesses at craft- and floral-supply stores. Proceed as follows:

1. Place one end of the wire into the flower before its edges are tacked together and the flower is wrapped. Stitch the wire end into the flower. (Figure 6.25.)

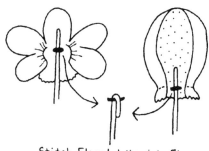

Stitch Floral Wire into Flower + Bend Top of Wire over Stitches

Fig. 6.25 *Place a wire stem into the flower while under construction. Tack it in place and bend the top over the stitching.*

2. Bend the end of the wire over the stitches that hold it. Finish the flower.

Attach felt leaves to the stem with glue or wrap them to the stem with matching thread. (Figure 6.26.)

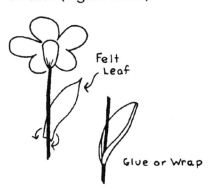

Felt Leaf

Glue or Wrap

Fig. 6.26 *Wrap or glue leaves to wire stems.*

Ribbon Stems

Where flowers are attached to a foundation fabric, let stems of narrow ribbon fall free from the flowers or tack them to the foundation in graceful meanders. For an interesting variation, tack ribbon to the foundation at regular intervals after wrapping it with thread to create little gathers. (Figure 6.27.)

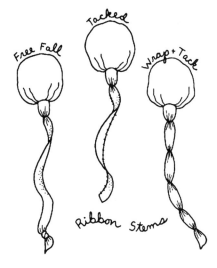

Fig. 6.27 *Ribbon stems can be allowed to take various forms. For the stem on the far right, wrap the tacking thread around the ribbon to gather before tacking to the foundation.*

Tack the ribbon stem into the flower as it is wrapped, so it becomes part of the flower's base. (Figure 6.28.)

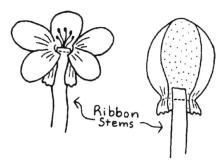

Fig. 6.28 *Tack ribbon stems in place in the flower's base while it is under construction.*

Flower Centers

Flower centers vary depending on the flower. For some, such as the rose, camellia, primrose, sweet pea, and dahlia, no center treatment is needed. Poppies and spring blossoms usually have stamens. Knotted daisies and sunflowers have disk-like centers.

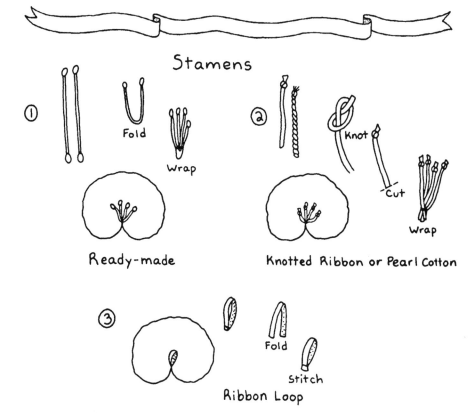

Fig. 6.29 *Stamens add a finishing touch to poppies and spring blossoms. Choose ribbon or thread stamens for washable uses.*

Stamens

Add stamens while the flower is under construction. (See Figures 6.10c, 6.16c on pages 66 and 68.) Use ribbon or pearl-cotton stamens for washables. Here are several alternatives. (Figure 6.29.)

1. *Ready-made stamens.* Fold them in half for shorter stamens. Wrap them together with thread before adding to the flower.

2. *Knotted ribbon or pearl cotton stamens.* Knot the end of a strand of 1/16"-wide yellow ribbon or #3 pearl cotton. Cut about 1" below the knot to make a short stamen. Wrap the stamens together with thread before adding to the flower.

3. *Ribbon loop.* For tiny flowers, such as mini poppies or spring blossoms, simply fold a little piece of 1/16"-wide yellow ribbon in half to make a loop. Tack the two ends together before adding it to the flower.

Disk Centers

Add a disk-like center after the flower is completed. Use one of these alternatives. (Figure 6.30.)

① Button

② Small Felt Circle

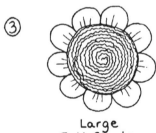

③ Large Felt Circle

Fig. 6.30 *Sunflowers and knotted daisies have disk-like centers.*

1. *A button.* Sew a large button in the center. Use a lightweight one so the center doesn't become too weighty.

2. *A small felt circle.* Use a small disk of yellow, green, brown, or orange felt in the center. Leave it plain or decorate with French knots (Figure

French Knot

Needle up. Wrap thread once or twice around needle.

Needle down at dot marked "x", while holding thread taut.

Fig. 6.31 *Making a French Knot.*

6.31) or seed beads. The knotted daisy shown in the color photographs has an orange felt center with brown French knots. For a decorated circle, mark the circle on a larger piece of felt, decorate, then cut it out.

3. *A large felt circle.* Decorate a large circle of felt by tacking a tight seam binding ruffle or a length of flat, narrow ribbon to it. Tack in a spiral pattern or randomly. This is the center used on the sunflower.

Finishing Flower Bases

Flowers often have raw ends at the base or back that need finishing. Leaves can be wrapped to the flower base before it is finished or added later. I usually prefer to wrap leaves with raw ends into the flower base before it is finished. This way, both flower and leaves receive a clean finish.

Add stems, if desired, before finishing the base.

To finish a base, first trim any stray threads from the base and even up the ribbon ends. If the base will not be visible, simply seal the raw ends with glue, using washable glue if necessary. If the base will show, there are three alternatives.

Base 1: Ribbon Base

a. Cut a length of ribbon to wrap around the base of the flower. Use a ribbon wide enough so the bottom edge of the ribbon extends below the base about 1/8" or 1/4". Turn under one end of the length and stitch across. Place glue

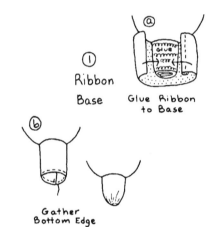

① Ribbon Base

ⓐ Glue Ribbon to Base

ⓑ Gather Bottom Edge

around the sides of the flower's base and wrap the ribbon around it.

b. Once dry, run a row of gathering stitches at the bottom edge of the ribbon. Pull up to encase the bottom of the flower's base in ribbon.

Base 2: Felt Base

a. Cut a length of felt similar to the ribbon for Base 1. Place glue on the sides of the flower's base and wrap the felt around it, overlapping the ends.

b. Once dry, line the inside of the felt that extends below the base with glue. Pinch the felt around the bottom of the base while the glue dries.

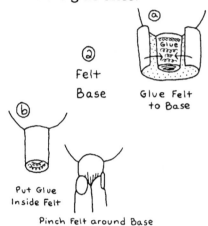

Felt
Base
Glue Felt
to Base
Put Glue
Inside Felt
Pinch Felt around Base

Base 3: Felt Circle Base

a. Cut a circle of felt about 1" – 1-1/2" in diameter, depending on the size of the flower. If the flower has a stem, cut a hole (wire stem) or slit (ribbon stem) in the center of the felt and place the stem through the opening. Place glue on the circle of felt.

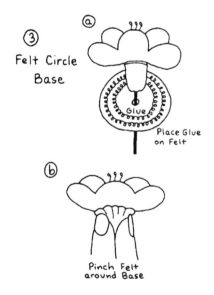

③
Felt Circle
Base
Glue
Place Glue
on Felt
Pinch Felt
around Base

b. Pinch the felt up around the sides of the base and let dry.

Leaves

Many flowers need a leaf or two to look complete. Ribbon or felt leaves are my preference, but ready-made silk leaves can also be used. Wire-edge taffeta makes beautiful leaves because they can be bent in graceful curves. Use ombré wire-edge taffeta for variegated leaves shaded from light to dark green, or from green to blue or mauve.

Stitch leaves to the base of a flower, or wrap them to the flower's base. They can also be wrapped or glued to stems. (See Figure 6.26 on page 72.)

Ribbon Leaves

This section displays ribbon leaf variations. Suggested ribbon widths and yardages are included in the directions for each leaf as starting points. Explore various widths for larger or smaller leaves.

Leaf 1

A bit of gathering gives this leaf a graceful, lifelike curve. Try satin or taffeta, especially wire-edge taffeta. Single-face ribbon is adequate. Sew the leaf to the back of a flower such as the camellia (page 65), or wrap it to the base of rolled roses or spring blossoms (pages 63 and 68).

    Small leaf: 4" of 5/8"-wide ribbon
    Larger leaf: 6" of 7/8"-wide ribbon

a. Fold the ribbon length in half crosswise, right sides together.

b. Hand stitch a line of running stitches from the end to the fold, in a shallow arc. Begin the stitching line halfway between the edges and end it at the right edge, near the fold.

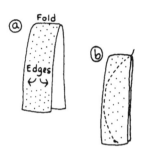

ⓐ Fold
Edges
ⓑ
ⓒ
ⓓ
Back View

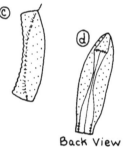

c. Pull up to gather until the stitching line is nearly straight.

d. Open out the leaf. On the back, tack the bottom of the seam open and the top fold down.

Leaf 2

Use this small leaf for tiny roses and clusters of roses. Use single-face satin ribbon. Wrap the leaf to the rose or cluster.

    Small Leaf: 2" of 7/8"-wide ribbon

a. With the wrong side of the ribbon up, fold the top corners to the center of the length.

Fold on dotted lines   Fold

b. Bring the two folds together.

c. Hand stitch a line of tiny gathering stitches, from the bottom right edge, diagonally to the midpoint on the folds.

d. Pull up to gather. Wrap the thread around the gathering line before ending it.

Leaf 3

Variation I   Variation 2

This leaf has two variations. Variation 1 makes a small leaf with no ribbon edges showing from the front. Variation 2 makes a larger leaf and incorporates the edges of the ribbon into the front of the leaf. Single-face ribbon, such as satin, is sufficient.

    Small leaf: 3-1/2" of 7/8"-
      wide ribbon
    Larger leaf: 5" of 1-1/2"-
      wide ribbon

a. Determine the midpoint of the ribbon length.
    Fold the top corners to the back so the top edges meet at the midpoint, forming a point.

Variation I

Variation 1: Work with the ribbon face up and fold the top corners to the back. Leave the ribbon ends next to each other.

Variation 2

Variation 2: Work with the ribbon wrong side up and fold the top corners to the front. Overlap the ribbon ends.

b. Stitch a row of gathering stitches:

Wrap

Variation 1: Stitch them at the bottom edge of the ribbon, catching in the folded-down ends.

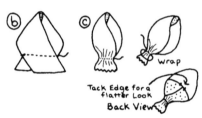
Tack Edge for a flatter Look
Back View   Wrap

Variation 2: Stitch them where the two ribbons cross each other.

c. Pull up the gathers and wrap the thread around the gathering line. For a flatter leaf on Variation 2, tack the back edge of the ribbon to the wrong side of the leaf front.

Leaf 4

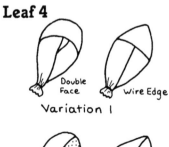
Double Face   Wire Edge
Variation I

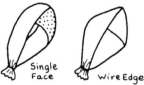
Single Face   Wire Edge
Variation 2

This is a good choice for large leaves. For a crisp look, use wire-edge taffeta and flatten the folds. For a softer look, use satin or grosgrain. In the color photographs, the red wire-edge camellia has flat, wire-edge leaves and the dahlia has soft, satin leaves. This leaf can be used with either side up. There are two ways to make the folds, each giving the leaf a slightly different effect. While this leaf is usually made with a double-face ribbon, I like the effect created with single-face satin showing its wrong side on the top right part of the point in variation 2.

    Medium leaf: 4" of 7/8"-
      wide ribbon
    Large leaf: 9" of 7/8"-wide
      ribbon
    Large, wide leaf: 8" – 9" of
      1-1/2"-wide ribbon

a. Fold the top edges of each end of the ribbon to the mid-point, forming a point.

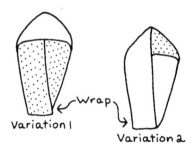
Variation I   Wrap   Variation 2

Variation 1: With right side up, fold both edges to the back.
Variation 2: With the wrong side of the ribbon up, fold one edge forward and one back.

b. Overlap the ends and wrap them tightly to gather the ribbon.

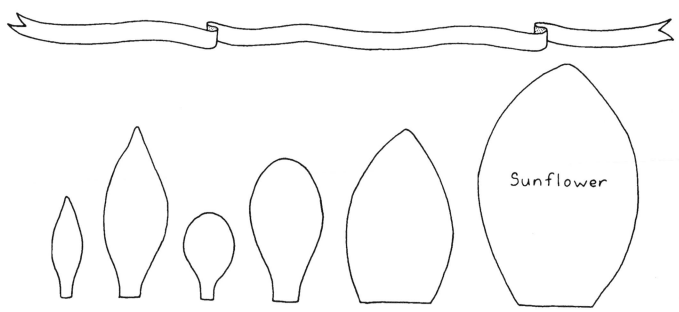

Fig. 6.32 *Patterns for felt leaves. For an interesting edge, cut out with pinking shears.*

Leaf 5

This actually makes a set of two large leaves on which a flower such as the primrose (see page 67) is placed. Use a double-face ribbon like grosgrain. Use either side of the leaf up.

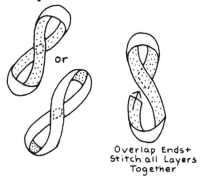

12" – 13" of 5/8"- or 7/8"-wide ribbon

a. Fold the ribbon into a figure 8, with the ends overlapping under the center intersection.

b. Stitch the ribbon layers together where they meet in the center.

Leaf 6

This set of two leaves is actually a gathered bow without the center wrap. It is pleasing in any size and complements imaginary flowers as well as realistic ones. Use green single-face satin and wire-edge taffeta, or experiment with other ribbons and colors.

Tiny leaf set: 3" of 3/8"-wide ribbon
Small leaf set: 5" of 5/8"-wide ribbon
Medium leaf set: 6" of 7/8"-wide ribbon
Large leaf set: 9-1/2" of 1-1/2"-wide ribbon

a. Bring the ends of a length of ribbon together. Overlap the ends and stitch.

b. With the overlap at center back, stitch two rows of gathering stitches in the center of the ribbon. Pull up to gather.

Felt Leaves

Figure 6.32 has patterns for leaves to cut from felt. Use pinking shears to add an interesting edge. Glue, wrap, or stitch them to a flower's base or to wire stems.

California Poppy T-Shirt ⏰⏰⏰

Make a T-shirt that is bound to turn heads with its bright colors. Draped among the poppies is a 3/8"-wide heat-set, wrinkled novelty ribbon. Look for several brands, including "Krinkle" by Hirschberg-Schutz and "Krunchie" by Offray. You may substitute 1/4"- or 3/8"-wide satin or grosgrain if you prefer.

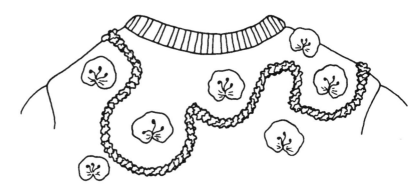

Fig. 6.33 *The California Poppy T-shirt boasts the state flower by scattering orange poppies around the top of a yellow shirt. A meandering length of green, wrinkled, novelty ribbon finishes the shirt.*

Supplies
1 bright yellow T-shirt without pocket
46" of 5/8"-wide orange grosgrain ribbon
1-1/4 – 2 yards of 3/8"-wide yellow-green wrinkled novelty ribbon (or one of the substitutes suggested above)
1 yard of 1/16"-wide yellow satin
Washable glue
Optional: Cardboard T-shirt board (available in fabric and craft stores)
Preshrink the T-shirt and ribbons.

a. Using 6-1/2" lengths of the orange ribbon, make five to seven poppies. (See Figure 6.10 on page 66.) Using the yellow ribbon, add three 1" long knotted ribbon stamens to each flower (see page 73).

Cut the raw ends on the finished flowers very short and seal them with washable glue.

b. Scatter the poppies around the top front of the T-shirt and pin them in place. Stitch them in place with blind stitches.

c. Randomly drape the green ribbon around the poppies and stitch to the shirt with matching thread. With satin or grosgrain, consider giving it texture by wrapping the thread around the ribbon as it is tacked to the shirt. This is similar to the treatment suggested for ribbon flower stems in Figure 6.27 on page 73.

Hint: To make the last two steps easier, put the T-shirt over a cardboard T-shirt board.

7. Ribbon Miscellany

Ribbon Weaving

Weave most any ribbon or combination of ribbons into motifs to dress up a sweatshirt, add a woven pattern piece to a garment, or add a pretty touch to a pocket or purse. To practice weaving, start with satin ribbon, 3/8" wide.

To make a finished piece of ribbon weaving easier to handle, weave over fusible interfacing; then fuse to keep the ribbons in place. Iron-on adhesive web can be used instead of interfacing so the weaving can be fused to the web, then fused to garments and such.

To make a woven shape, or create a woven garment part, first make a woven rectangle large enough to accommodate the shape, then after fusing it, cut it out.

After the shape is cut, there will be lots of raw ends. Finish the edges of applied shapes with machine applique or dimensional fabric paints. For pattern pieces, overcast or otherwise finish the raw ends. Consider lining the piece.

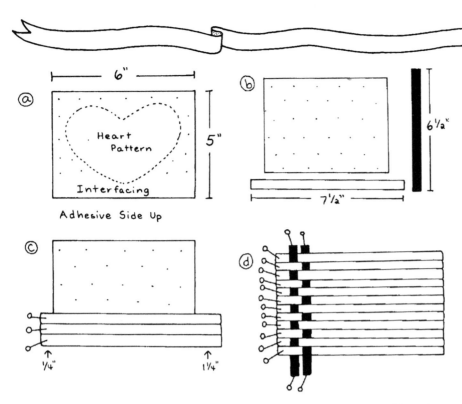

Fig. 7.1 *Weave ribbon over fusible interfacing. Pin the horizontal lengths in place (c), then weave and pin the vertical lengths in place (d). Once the weaving is complete, fuse it to the interfacing.*

Here is the technique for ribbon weaving. Refer to Figure 7.1. The instructions produce a woven rectangle of a size that will accommodate a heart made with the pattern in Figure 3.26 on page 34.

a. Determine the size of the rectangle needed to accommodate the shape. Don't skimp. For the heart in Figure 3.26, a 5" x 6" rectangle should be sufficient.

Cut a 5" x 6" rectangle from fusible interfacing. Place it adhesive side up on a *press* board (not a foam-board pin board) or ironing board.

b. Determine the length of the ribbon needed for weaving.

Allow the ribbon to be at least 1" longer than the rectangle to allow some ease for ribbon taken up in the weaving. When weaving a large piece allow more than 1".

For this rectangle, make the vertical ribbons at least 6-1/2" long and the horizontal ones 7-1/2" long.

c. Cut sufficient horizontal strips to cover the interfacing. Pin them in place across the interfacing so each overhangs the interfacing by 1/4" on the left side. Place a pin in this 1/4" overhang.

d. Cut sufficient vertical strips to cover the interfacing. Weave them over and under the horizontal strips, placing the first strip at the left edge of the interfacing. Pin the strips at the top and bottom to hold them in place.

Carefully remove the pins from the bottom of the vertical strips. Fuse the interfacing to the weaving according to the manufacturer's directions. Cover the ribbon with a press cloth before fusing to protect the ribbon.

e. Cut the heart shape from the rectangle, if desired.

Woven Ribbon Greeting Card ♀♀♀

Fig. 7.2 *Make personalized woven ribbon greeting cards.*

Fig. 7.3 *Cut a shape in the paper that will be the top of the card. Attach a rectangle of woven ribbon to the paper that will be the back of the card. Hold the front and back together with double-sided tape.*

Make a very special greeting card with ribbon weaving. Rather than cut a shape from ribbon, cut a pretty shape window in the card and place a rectangle of woven ribbons behind it. For the 5" x 6" Valentine's Day card in the color photographs, I wove a rectangle of pink feather-edge satin and white scallop-edge novelty ribbon. The card is made of rough surface watercolor paper; a sturdy paper with interesting texture. I cut a heart-shape window in the card and finished the card by writing a personal greeting and drawing a lace-like decoration around the heart. You may also want to decorate with stickers, rubber stamps, ribbon, lace, or glitter.

Refer to Figure 7.3.

a. Cut out a rectangle for the card front from the desired paper. Cut a second piece, a little smaller, for a backing. Cut the desired shape window into the card front. Decorate the front of the card.

b. Weave a rectangle of ribbon large enough for the window. Weave over fusible interfacing.

c. Glue the woven ribbon rectangle to the backing so it will show through the window. Hold the card front and backing together with double-sided tape or glue.

Woven Ribbon Variation:

Pointed-Edge Weaving

Finish the edges on a weaving with points. To practice this technique we will make a basket motif. (Figure 7.4.) Fill

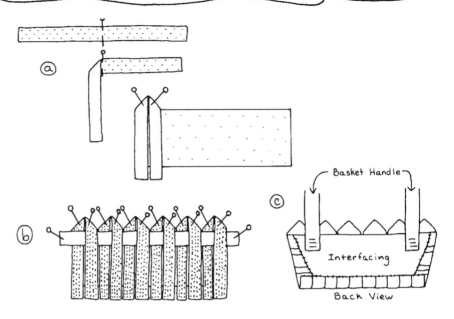

Fig. 7.4 This basket motif, adapted from an early ribbon text, looks just as inviting today as it did then. Fill the basket with tiny ribbon flowers.

the basket with flowers or other treasures of your choosing, then attach it to a pocket or shirt.

Small spring blossoms (see page 68) made of seam binding fill the basket in Figure 7.4.

Fig. 7.5 Make the basket over fusible interfacing. a. Fold and pin the pointed vertical pieces in place. b. Weave the horizontal lengths. c. Turn the raw ends at the sides and bottom to the back. Add the handle.

Supplies

6 pieces of 3/8"-wide satin, 5" long (Color 1)
3 pieces of 3/8"-wide satin, 5-1/2" long (Color 2)
7" of 3/8"-wide satin, Color 1 or 2 (for handle)
4" x 1-1/2" piece of fusible interfacing

Refer to Figure 7.5.

a. Place the interfacing adhesive side up on a press board or ironing board.

Fold the ends of the 5" pieces of Color 1, to form a point.

Pin these across the top of the interfacing so the points are above the interfacing.

b. Weave in the 5-1/2" pieces of Color 2, letting the ribbon overhang the left edge by 1/2". Pin into this overhang.

Cover the ribbon with a press cloth and fuse the ribbon to the interfacing, also pressing the points flat.

c. Fold the raw ends on the sides to the back, at an angle. (See Figure 7.5.) Blind stitch the ends to the interfacing.

Fold the raw ends at the bottom to the back just below the last horizontal ribbon length. Blind stitch the ends to the interfacing.

Attach the ribbon handle to the basket, tacking the ends to the back of the basket.

Attach the motif to a fabric foundation with a blind hem.

Fill the basket with miniature flowers or other treasures.

A Ribbon Button

Fashion pieces of ribbon into three-dimensional buttons that look like miniature pyramids. (Figure 7.6.) Use them to decorate the center of rosettes, bows, and bands of ribbon. Make earrings with them. Use one to cover the overlap of ends on a ribbon band. Use a sturdy, double-face ribbon such as grosgrain. Have a threaded needle with matching thread ready to finish off the button.

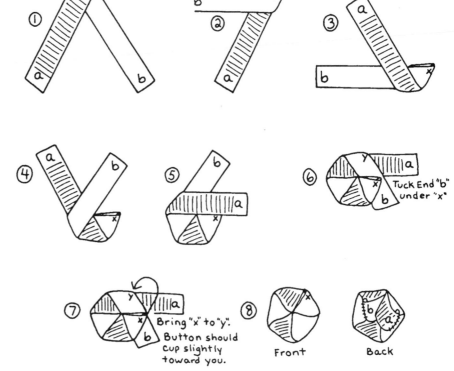

Fig. 7.7 Making a ribbon button.

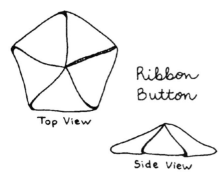

Fig. 7.6 Ribbon buttons stand up like little pyramids.

Small button: 5" of 3/8"-wide grosgrain

Medium button: 8-1/2" of 5/8"-wide grosgrain

Large button: 11" of 7/8"-wide grosgrain

Refer to Figure 7.7.

1. Fold the ribbon in half, as shown, so ends "a" and "b" are of equal length.

2. Fold end "b" over end "a", so the edge of "b" is against the fold made in the previous step.

3. Fold end "a" over end "b".

4. Fold end "b" over end "a".

5. Fold end "a" over end "b".

6. Fold end "b" over end "a", and tuck end "b" under the starting point marked "x".

7. Bring point "x" to meet point "y". Tack the two together invisibly. The button should cup slightly into a little pyramid.

8. Turn under both ends on the back of the button and stitch in place.

Knotted Ribbon

Fig. 7.8 Knotted ribbon adds a playful finish.

Knotted
Fringe

Knot pieces of ribbon and use them to make fringe to decorate baskets, mats, pockets, and other clothing details. (Figure 7.8.) The mat under the bow tree shown in the color photographs has a knotted ribbon edging.

Knot ribbon lengths with an overhand knot. (Figure 7.9a.) Cut the knotted end on a diagonal to retard fraying. (Figure 7.9b.)

Make a rolled tulle flower (see page 65) and finish it with knotted ribbon streamers instead of leaves. (Figure 7.10.) Use these as party favors or hostess gifts.

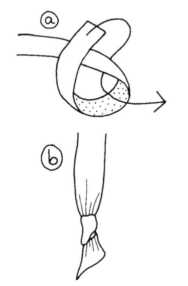

ⓐ

ⓑ

Fig. 7.9 Knot the end of lengths of ribbon and cut the end on a diagonal to retard fraying.

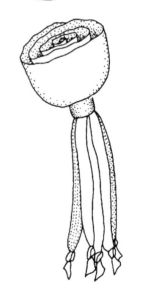

Fig. 7.10 Instead of leaves, add knotted ribbon streamers to flowers.

The Icing on the Cake ☺☺☺☺☺

Well, there you have it. You are now a ribbon master! Celebrate by making and decorating a cake with ribbon frosting.

On the cover and in the color photographs is an 8-1/2" round cake with 4" high sides made of heavy watercolor paper with corrugated cardboard braces. It is decorated with pleated grosgrain and satin, a grosgrain band, and satin rolled roses and leaves. Use it as a centerpiece for family birthdays.

In the color photographs is another cake, made from a 6" round balsa wood box with lid (available at craft stores) that has been covered with watercolor paper. It is decorated with a flat ribbon rose, shell ruffle, and various bands of satin and grosgrain. These make welcome birthday gifts for friends trying to watch their calories. Hide other presents inside the box.

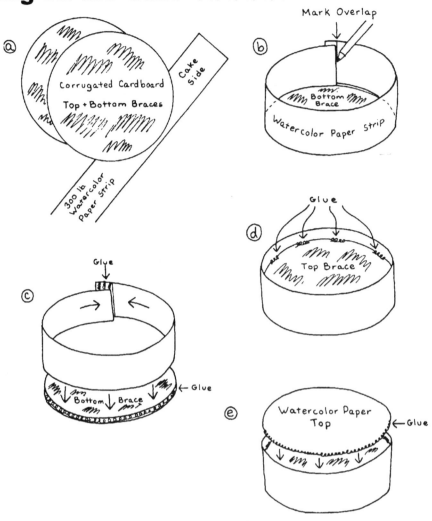

Fig. 7.12 Make the paper cake from 300 lb. watercolor paper, with cardboard braces in the top and bottom.

The 8-1/2" Cake

Fig. 7.11 Decorate a paper cake with ribbon icing for a unique table decoration.

The watercolor paper and corrugated cardboard can be cut with a pair of large all-purpose scissors. The size of the watercolor sheet may seem big but it must be so to have sufficient length to make the cake's sides.

Supplies
22" x 30" sheet of 300-lb. rough-surface watercolor paper
Corrugated cardboard sufficient for two 8-1/2" circles (for interior braces)
White glue
Ribbons and other decorations

Refer to Figure 7.12.

a. Using a dinner plate about 8-1/2" around as a pattern, draw two circles on corrugated cardboard. Cut out these circles.

Wrap a tape measure around the perimeter of one of the cardboard circles to determine the size for the side strip. Add 1" so the ends of the strip can overlap. Determine how high the cake sides will be, and cut the side strip from the watercolor paper. The side strip for the cake pictured measures 4" x 28".

b. Wrap the watercolor paper strip around the bottom brace and mark the overlap of its ends with a pencil. Mark it all the way across the strip.

c. Put white glue on the edge of the bottom brace and on the marked overlap area. Glue the side strip to the bottom brace and hold the overlap pieces together until the glue will hold on its own. Let the glue dry thoroughly.

d. Fit the top brace into the top of the cake. It should fit snugly, but not so tight that it distorts the cake's sides. Trim it if needed. Push it about 1" down into the cake. Attach it to the cake sides with short lines of glue that touch the inside of the watercolor paper strip and the edge of the top brace. Let the glue dry thoroughly.

e. Using the unfinished cake as a pattern, cut a circle from the watercolor paper to fit the top of the cake. The circle should touch the sides of the cake with no overhang. Put glue around the edge of the watercolor paper circle. Place it on top of the cake. Wipe off any excess glue, but don't worry about a little glue showing here since the edge will be covered with ribbon decoration. Let the glue dry thoroughly.

f. Decorate the cake lavishly.

The Cake Box

Supplies

6" round, 2-1/2"-high balsa wood box with lid
16" x 20" sheet of 140-lb. rough-surface watercolor paper
White glue
Ribbons and other decorations

Refer to Figure 7.13.

a. Place the lid on the wooden box. Use a pencil to lightly draw a line around the side of the box at the place where the bottom of the lid sits on it. This will later be a guide for cutting the side strip of paper.

b. Cover the lid: Cut a circle from the watercolor paper to fit the top of the lid. Measure the width of the side of the lid. Add 1/8" – 1/4" to this measurement so the paper covering the lid will hang down below the wood. Measure around the perimeter of the lid. Add 1" for the ends of the strip to overlap. Cut a strip of watercolor paper to the measurements.

Place a ring of glue on the wooden top, just inside the edge. Lay the paper circle on top so the glue holds it in place. Wipe any excess glue from the edge.

Glue the side strip to the lid, gluing only where the ends overlap. Let the glue dry thoroughly.

c. Cover the sides of the box: Measure the perimeter of the box. Add 1" for the ends of the strip to overlap. Measure from the bottom of the box to the pencil line marked in Step "a". This is the width of the strip. Cut a side strip from watercolor paper.

Wrap the strip around the box. On many wood boxes, the lids do not fit quite evenly and the strip will need to be trimmed to match the pencil mark in some places. This edge will be covered by the overhang on the lid, so any unevenness due to trimming will not show.

Glue the side strip to the box using glue only on the overlap. Let the glue dry thoroughly.

d. Decorate the box and lid.

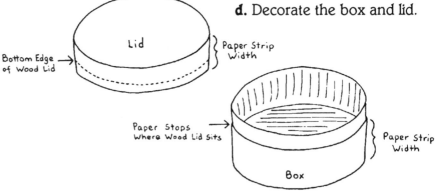

Fig. 7.13 Cover the balsa wood box and lid with 140 lb. watercolor paper. Let the paper strip on the sides of the lid overhang the wood a bit. Cover the sides of the box only to the point where the bottom of the lid sits. Decorate with ribbon icing details. Hide a present inside the box.

Sources of Supply

Equipment and Notions

Check local fabric, needlework, and craft supply stores for the equipment and notions mentioned in the book. Also write for the catalogs from these mail-order companies.

Clotilde
1909 S.W. First Ave.
Ft. Lauderdale, FL 33315
305-761-8655
1-800-772-2891 (orders only)

Perfect Pleater, all kinds of sewing notions, ironing aids, stabilizers, and adhesives, plus books, videos, and two colorful ribbon assortment packages (Amish and Pastel).

Nancy's Notions
P.O. Box 683
Beaver Dam, WI 53916-0683
414-887-0391
1-800-833-0690 (orders only)

A wide variety of sewing notions and supplies, including stabilizers and adhesives. Also patterns and videos.

Newark Dressmakers Supply
P.O. Box 20730
Lehigh Valley, PA 18002
215-837-7500

Sewing notions and supplies, plus some ribbons, laces and trims.

Treadleart
25834-I Narbonne Ave.
Lomita, CA 90717
310-534-5122
800-327-4222 (orders only)

Sewing supplies, machine embroidery threads, stabilizers, adhesives, books, and patterns. Ribbons are available in the retail store at the above address. Catalog: $3.00 (refundable).

Woven-Edge Ribbon Sources

Most fabric and craft stores carry a wide variety of ribbons. Look to them for your basic ribbon needs. For imported and vintage ribbons, look to the sources listed below or ask your local store to contact one of the companies listed below as a wholesale source.

Angelsea
P.O. Box 4586
Stockton, CA 95204
209-948-8428

Mail-order. Catalog is $3.00 and comes with discount coupons. Vast assortment of beautiful imported ribbons, trims, and flowermaking supplies such as leaves and stamens.

Britex Fabrics
146 Geary St.
San Francisco, CA 94108
415-392-2910

Retail store. A must-see, four-storey fantasy. The fourth floor is devoted to ribbons, trims, and notions. Complete selection of imported and domestic ribbons.

Elsie's Exquisiques
208 State St.
St. Joseph, MI 49085
616-982-0449

Retail store. Wide array of unusual ribbons, trims, and handmade ribbon flowers and leaves. Direct importer of silk ribbons and reproduction trims. Wholesale catalog available to retailers.

Home Sew
P.O. Box 4099
Bethlehem, PA 18018
215-867-3833

Mail-order. Free catalog. A variety of ribbons, trims, laces, and notions. Interesting assortment packages of ribbons and trims, and a Sample Club.

Judith Designs
P.O. Box 177
Castle Rock, CO 80104

Mail-order. Catalog $1.50. Silk ribbons and threads for embroidery, books, laces, buttons, beads, and doodads. Owner is Judith Montano (see Bibliography).

Ribbon Outlet
1-800-766-BOWS (2697)

Retail stores nationwide, with a large selection of ribbon varieties and a vast color range in basic ribbons such as satin and grosgrain. Also trims and laces. Mail orders are handled through stores. Call them for the location of a store near you.

The Ribbonry
119 Louisiana Ave.
Perrysburg, OH 43551
419-872-0073

Retail shop and mail-order. Call or write for catalog cost. Imported French ribbons and custom-made ribbon items.

Tail of the Yak
2632 Ashby Ave.
Berkeley, CA 94705
415-841-9891

Retail store carrying a wide variety of vintage ribbons and other indescribable pleasures. Featured in the January 1993 issue of "Victoria" magazine.

Viv's Ribbons and Laces
212 Virginia Hills Dr.
Martinez, CA 94553
510-933-7758

Mail-order retail and wholesale. Catalog $3.50. Silk ribbon, imported laces, specialty ribbons and braids.

Y.L.I. Corporation
P.O. Box 109
Provo, UT 84603-0109
801-377-3900
800-854-1932 (orders only)

Mail-order retail and wholesale. Catalog $1.50. Complete range of Japanese silk ribbons from 2mm – 32mm wide (1/16" – 1-1/4" approx.) for ribbon work and embroidery, silk ribbon embroidery books, interesting ribbon trims.

Ribbon Manufacturers

The companies listed below supply woven-edge ribbon. Many also supply craft ribbons suitable for the techniques in this book. Contact them for the nearest shop that carries their ribbons. Send a stamped, self-addressed envelope for reply.

Grayblock Ribbon Mills
P.O. Box 967
Easton, MD 21601
301-822-6100

Complete line of woven-edge ribbons, including a wide variety of picot-edge ribbons and ribbons with woven-in patterns.

Hirschberg-Schutz Co.
565 Green Lane
Union, NJ 07083
908-352-4800
800-221-8640 (wholesale inquiries only)

"Krinkles" brand heat-set wrinkled novelty ribbon. They are not set up to handle inquiries from individuals, but give their address and telephone number to your local store so they can order.

Lion Ribbon Company
Route 24, Box 601
Chester, NJ 07930-0601
908-879-4700

Complete line of craft ribbons, including beautiful wire-edge taffetas, tulles, and holiday ribbons.

C.M. Offray & Son, Inc.
Route 24, Box 601
Chester, NJ 07930-0601
908-879-4700

In addition to the basics, ribbons with interesting contemporary and children's patterns. A wonderful array of woven-edge novelties and special-occasion ribbons, such as bridal. Look for their "Make It With Ribbons" pamphlet series where the ribbons are sold.

Sopp America, Inc.
1 Chris Ct.
Dayton, NJ 08810
908-274-2225
800-233-2697

A variety of craft ribbons, including holiday themes, for bows and other craft uses.

William E. Wright
85 South Street
West Warren, MA 01092
413-436-7732

All of the basics in a wonderful array of colors and widths. Beautiful satins. Also complete lines of seam binding, pleated ribbon, and trims. Look for their craft pamphlets where the ribbons and trims are sold.

Lectures and Workshops

Please include a stamped, self-addressed envelope for reply.

Ceci Johnson
174 Cindy Ave.
Clovis, CA 93612

Workshops on contemporary ribbon techniques and projects.

Candace Kling
127 Monte Cresta Avenue
Oakland, CA 94611

Lectures and workshops on vintage ribbon techniques.

Bibliography

Anderson, Kay, *Fashion with Ribbon*, B.T. Batsford, Ltd., London, England, 1987.
Ideas for weaving ribbon for clothing and accessories.

The Art and Craft of Ribbonwork, Vol. 1 & 2. Reprint by Body Blueprints, 1734 Scott St., St. Helena, CA 94574.
Reprint of a 1921 text on ribbonwork with techniques and pictures of ribbon used on items popular at the time.

Betzina, Sandra, "20th-Century Ribbon Sculptress Candace Kling," *Threads Magazine,* August/September 1987 issue.

Dodson, Jackie, *Know Your Sewing Machine,* Chilton Book Company, Radnor, PA, 1988.
A good overview of machine techniques. Also available are "Know Your..." titles covering specific brands of machines.

Evans, Hilary, *Ribbonwork,* Bobbs-Merrill, New York, 1976.
Out of print. Contemporary ribbon uses.

Kaye, Georgina Kerr, *Millinery for Every Woman,* John C. Winston Co., 1926, Reprinted 1992 by Lacis, 3163 Adeline St., Berkeley, CA 94703.
An extensive section on making flowers from ribbon and fabric.

Kling, Candace, "Decorative Ribbon Work", *Threads Magazine*, August/September 1987 issue.

Candace Kling's ribbon artistry is a treasure. See it in the Betzina article mentioned above, the Spring 1992 issue of Treasures in Needlework, *and the June and December 1991 issues of* Victoria *magazine. Also in a video called* Wearable Art From California: Ellen Hauptli *and Candace Kling. (write: University of California, Extension Media Center, 2176 Shattuck Ave., Berkeley CA 94704.)*

McNeill, Suzanne, *Basic Bows,* Design Originals, 1992, Booklet #1031.
Colorful, contemporary bow ideas.

Montano, Judith, *Crazy Quilt Odyssey,* C&T Publishing, Lafayette, CA, 1991.
Subtitled, "Adventures in Victorian Needlework." A book of inspiration on using ribbons and other treasures in crazy quilting.

Perez-Collins, Yvonne, *Soft Gardens,* Chilton Book Company, Radnor, PA, 1993.
Contemporary flower techniques, including the use of ribbon.

Ribbon Art Publishing, *Old Fashioned Ribbon Art,* Dover Publications, New York, 1986.
Ideas for vintage ribbon projects.

Saunders, Jan, *Step-by-Step Guide to Your Sewing Machine,* Chilton Book Company, Radnor, PA, 1990.
A good text on the use of the sewing machine. Also available are "Step-by-Step..." titles for specific brands of machines.

Shaeffer, Claire, *Claire Shaeffer's Fabric Sewing Guide,* Chilton Book Company, Radnor, PA, 1989.
Wonderful reading. Everything you need to know about fabrics. Good sections on sewing techniques.

Sienkiewicz, Elly, *Dimensional Appliqué—Baskets, Blooms, and Baltimore Borders,* C&T Publishing, Lafayette, CA, 1993.

—, "Flowers from Baltimore Album Quilts," *Threads Magazine,* December 1992/January 1993 issue.

Sirkis, Susan, *The Art of Ribboncraft,* video, available from: Concept Associates, 7910 Woodmont Ave., Suite 1214, Bethesda, MD 20814.

A good overview of ribbon techniques, especially using silk ribbons.

Thompson, Sue, *Decorative Dressmaking,* Rodale Press, Emmaus, PA, 1985.
Inspiration in creative clothing decoration. Out of Print, but worth the hunt to find.

Women's Institute of Domestic Arts & Sciences, *Ribbon Trimmings: A Course in Six Parts,* Sloane Publications, 1992.
Reprint of a 1922 text covering all aspects of ribbon work. Impressive amount of information. Order from Viv's Ribbons & Laces (See Sources of Supply).

Index